This book is dedicated to my Grandmother

Lily Wilson

who taught me everything about

hard work and being resilient.

D1556125

0

<u>Contents</u>

Introduction

As I sit down to start writing this book in my office overlooking Belfast's famous shipyard, the sun is shining over my beautiful home city and I am feeling incredibly optimistic today.

Two things are very significant to me.

Firstly, it's my 46th birthday.

Secondly, one in five people across the entire planet is currently locked down in their homes to prevent the spread of a lethal viral pandemic.

Astonishingly, the world's economy is on pause.

The lives and movements of millions of people are restricted indefinitely.

Doom and fear currently dominate every news headline and conversation, and the future is one of total uncertainty.

In terms of health and the economy, this is the worst thing that has happened since the Second World War.

But it's a global problem that I have no control over.

I have total faith that the medical experts will quickly come up with a solution.

We need to live with and then beat the Coronavirus – we cannot let the virus destroy us.

I need to tend and protect my small patch of the world.

I accept this crisis has its own energy, so I don't need to give it any of mine.

I have decided to control my juggernaut of energy and keep it on a trajectory for personal fulfilment and daily self-belief.

So today of all days, why do I feel so happy and prosperous?

Well, it's not just because of the birthday wishes and gifts I have received from family and friends, (although I'm very grateful for those).

Nor is it because I am in denial of the changing reality of the world under siege to a virus.

No, I am feeling positive because, for me, the crisis is already over.

I'm looking at the far horizon and imagining a new dawn beyond the present darkness.

I can see past not just the immediate issues such as business closures, staff layoffs and complex logistics, but two steps beyond the fall-out.

I am 100 per cent confident that opportunities for personal and professional fulfilment will abound again.

In economic terms, after any downturn, there is always a massive boom – and I am planning for that period of future prosperity.

Belfast's constant rejuvenation underpins my optimism.

I've learned that you need to be able to imagine a better future before you can make it happen.

You must cultivate resilience to forge ahead and smash any obstacles.

Even when you feel flattened by circumstances - and your own actions - and hit rock bottom, it is possible to bounce back up even stronger and wiser than before.

As any champion boxer will tell you - it's not how hard you can hit, it's how you get back up again that counts.

But you need to really believe you can take the punches and not just survive but flourish.

Of course, you would be a fool to step into a boxing ring without the proper training to build resilience and skills before you face the challenge.

Otherwise, you will simply throw in the towel at the first blow and never pick yourself up again.

Good boxers need good trainers.

They rely on someone to advise them, counsel them and actually drive them on to success.

They need a trustworthy and experienced friend literally in their corner.

Doesn't everyone?

And that is what I am going to be for you.

In this book, I am going to share my personal secrets of positive thinking, proactive productivity and programmed resilience for personal reinvention.

I will be your guide, teacher, mentor, friend and motivator.

Based on my own journey from adversity through to global success, I'm going to share insights, stories and secrets that will both entertain and educate you.

I have climbed from having zero to owning a globally-successful, award-winning hospitality and property business with successful companies in Ireland, the UK, Europe, Asia, South America and the Middle East.

I have learned through adversity and gratitude, failure and success, that life is a game. But with my help, you can load the dice firmly in your favour with a few simple shifts in thinking and acting.

Suppose you want to have a more prosperous and productive experience in everything you do. In that case, this is the perfect moment to step up to the plate and commit to change.

Now is the time to cast off what has been holding you back, recalibrate your life and map out a new path that leads forward and upward. I have already walked that road, so I can help you find your way.

Now is the time to imagine a better future and create a structured plan to achieve it. I turned my dream into a fantastic reality, and I am going to support you to do the same.

I'm often asked how I have achieved the success I enjoy today.

I also own multiple high-turnover businesses, including one of the UK's biggest and fastest-growing serviced apartments companies with over 300 design-led apartments in major UK urban hubs, including Liverpool, Newcastle, Manchester, Middlesbrough, as well as internationally in Paris, Barcelona, Amsterdam and Sao Paulo.

I had the honour and pleasure of literally changing the landscape of my city and its local tourist industry by creating, building and growing my company - Dream Luxury Serviced Apartments.

This ever-expanding business has been the realisation of my dream, (hence the name).

The incredible success is a huge personal and professional achievement for me.

At the 2019 World Travel Awards, Dream Luxury Serviced Apartments in Belfast was awarded the title of 'Northern Ireland's Leading Serviced Apartments' for the third consecutive year.

With Dream Luxury Serviced Apartments, I introduced a new concept in luxury, short-term accommodation and hospitality in Belfast and other major cities.

I opened a whole new market sector and set the very highest standards for serviced apartments anywhere in the world.

I am so proud that Dream Luxury Serviced Apartments creates employment and career opportunities and brings increased wealth to my city.

I have dedicated my career to setting the benchmark for quality, and I believe Belfast has the potential to be a global leader in the hospitality and tourism sectors.

Dream Luxury Serviced Apartments is the realisation of my initial vision for changing the way people use and engage with the hospitality and short-term accommodation sector.

And now, it is a reality with thousands of people from all over the world using our services on a daily basis.

I first encountered the serviced apartment sector whilst on business in Dubai, and this is where I fell in love with the concept. It had never really been done before on a big scale in my home city, and I thought to myself 'why not?'

In a light bulb moment of inspiration, I knew I had found a viable alternative to the traditional hotel offering.

I also knew that flashbulb had to be intensified into a focused spotlight to turn my vision into reality.

This is the point where too often great projects fall apart and fail to materialise - because they are trapped in the imagination without action and momentum to actualise them.

Don't worry; I am going to reveal to you in this book how never to let this happen to you again.

On returning to Belfast from the Middle East, I realised there was an opportunity for top-quality serviced apartments to flourish in the Northern Irish tourism scene.

Nobody had done it before because nobody had questioned the current reality.

Things had just always been that way. The power and ownership of city centre tourism and business accommodation had for decades been owned by a small group of long-established hotel players.

My vision was a 'disruptor' concept to the established market.

So I needed courage and self-belief to cut a new path and invest in what was an untested concept in Belfast.

I possessed the vision and faith but required decisive action to make my dream a reality. So I created the opportunity to partner with an established serviced apartment provider from London and expanded my knowledge of the industry.

So what exactly drives my desire always to do better, go farther and be exceptional?

Let me level with you - I wasn't born under a lucky star.

I didn't have any advantages over you in terms of education or financial background.

I don't have superhuman powers, and I didn't sign a deal with the devil.

In fact, the circumstances of my upbringing in Belfast, as I'm going to tell you in this book, probably disadvantaged me in many ways.

Although, growing up there has also inspired me to greater heights.

My point is - if I can do it, you can too.

I'm using the story of my home city of Belfast to prove that you can overcome any adversity.

You can scale the most incredible heights - regardless of your starting point.

To borrow a phrase from Sinatra, if you can make it there, i.e. Belfast, you can make it anywhere! It's up to you.

As I sit and reflect on the old world disintegrating due to COVID-19, I'm stopping to take stock before the new reality kicks in.

I'm considering how and why I achieved this level of success. Though it is worth noting as it may provide a clue - I am not writing this book now because I have time on my hands waiting on the world to restart.

I'm writing it to prove a point.

In fact, I have never been busier. As I said, I am visualising the time beyond this crisis, laying plans and making deals for the future.

Forget horizon-scanning; I'm using a high-powered telescope to see what's ahead to offer opportunities for me to build my empire.

I'm already preparing to navigate the new reality ahead. I'm not getting bogged down in the current mire of negativity.

I've been thinking about what has driven me to achieve so much, especially in the face of adversity?

Having retraced my steps back through the journey of my life, I have identified the tools and techniques that allowed me to progress.

I have put them together in this book, along with insights and personal experiences and stories, so that I can share my learning with you.

I am going to tell you the story of how I was born into a working-class area of Belfast at the start of a four-decade-long civil war.

And how I went from working in a local fast-food outlet aged just 10-years-old, to establishing and growing a number of successful property companies.

This book is a rollercoaster ride through turbulent times in Northern Irish history and it's peppered with the good, the bad and the ugly.

It's a history lesson and a street-psychology lecture, animated by a personal narrative of fearlessness in the face of extreme circumstances in the 80s and 90s in Belfast. I have learned, through hard-won experience, tough cities deliver tough life lessons.

But these can be channelled positively to fuel both personal and professional goals.

So I am going to explain to you how I achieved exceptional levels of health, wealth and personal satisfaction. It must be remembered that exceptional people live the same lives and face the same challenges as everyone else.

But what sets them apart are their agile and resilient responses and how they use their personal skills to navigate the inevitable roadblocks.

The good news is that a goal-orientated mindset can be developed through learning and practice.

I believe mindset is the fundamental secret to my success.

I am not going to lie to you; this is not going to be easy.

If it were, everyone would have exceptional financial and business success.

But it is achievable if you work and apply yourself with full and dedicated commitment.

Your effort will result in proportionate rewards. Put massive effort in, and you will get massive rewards.

If you sell yourself short through laziness or lack of confidence, your rewards will decrease.

It's that simple. But it is also that difficult.

So I am going to guide you and help you develop the core strengths of determination, regeneration, energisation, ambition and motivation to turn your dreams into a reality.

These key DREAM words will be the five rungs of the ladder to propel you upward - but you are going to have to stretch to reach them and practice to get a firm footing.

Through my unique program, I'm going to teach you how to be exceptional by sharing the secrets of my success.

But you must recognise that it requires you to change.

You will need to reset your goals and refocus your vision to point beyond the usual horizon line.

You will need to imagine yourself as someone different to who you are today, be willing to break out of your comfort zone and reprogram.

Only you know your true potential, but you need to DREAM bigger to achieve better and learn how to maintain that momentum to sustain your pre-destined success.

Today is my birthday, but in a role reversal, I am going to give you the greatest gift you will ever receive!   I'm going to personally empower you to be the very best version of yourself every day.

I guarantee you will benefit from my unique DREAM formula as you discover the power of transformation from within your mind.

If you want to achieve your dreams, all you need to do is read on...

"It's the possibility of having a dream come true that makes life interesting." - Paulo Coelho

Tom Smyth's Five Principles of Dream to Achieve

Chapter 1: Determination

Chapter 2: Regeneration

Chapter 3: Energisation

Chapter 4: Ambition

Chapter 5: Motivation

What is Tom Smyth's DREAM system?

To accomplish your long term goals, you must want to be successful as much as you want to breathe.

Let me begin by thanking you for picking up my book and investing your time and effort into learning to live by my tried and tested DREAM system.

I am going to repay your faith in me by giving you my five keys to success.

These are the core principles of how I live my life and how I have achieved both personal and business success.

I am also going to share with you some of my own experiences, years of learning and advice I have received from some of the world's greatest success stories.

While I have done some of the graft for you already, you are going to have put in hard work if you want to reap the benefits.

I wasn't born the Tom Smyth I am today.

I had to create the person I wanted to be.

Every day I keep reinventing myself as a better person with bigger ambitions and desires.

As we go through this book, we are working as a team. I am going to be your personal coach to help you achieve your full potential.

Getting to the top of my profession and enjoying all the material reward that brings has not been an easy ride for me.

I'm not smarter, luckier or more privileged than you or anyone else.

You could say I started at a disadvantage being born in war-torn Northern Ireland.

But I believe that difficult start worked to my advantage because I had to struggle harder than most people to achieve my dreams.

The title of this book is a tribute to Belfast and all it has taught me about cultivating resilience.

Like a phoenix, Belfast has risen many times from the ashes through sheer force of will and belief that it could always be better.

It has weathered the storms of changing industrial trends, economic downturns, wartime bombing, poverty and even a 30-year civil war.

And yet, here it proudly sits on the banks of the Lagan enjoying its prosperity.

It's not the architecture or the bricks and mortar that are unbreakable in Belfast, but rather the spirit of its people.

They have always been hard-working and resolute in their determination, never to be beaten.

Belfast's story should be a great inspiration for you as well.

Its modern success story and increasing global status is clear proof that no challenge is insurmountable.

A few decades ago, it would have been unimaginable that Belfast would become a tourist hot spot packed with world-class restaurants, shops and entertainment.

The lesson for you in this story is that it does not matter where or how you start.

It only matters that you do start.

So begin with a blank slate.

Free yourself from the past which has been holding you back.   It's over, and you can't change it.

Embrace previous failures and learn from them.   Harness them to become a strength.

For example, during The Troubles, Belfast famous murals were seen as intimidating territory markers.   They were shown on the international news as a visual sign of the city's violent circumstances.

Now those same murals are a popular tourist attraction!

Local entrepreneurs have built a business on them as they take foreign visitors on bus and taxi tours of the former conflict zones.

If the will and work are there, that's the sort of incredible transformation that is possible.

So relax and be confident that if you put the effort in, every situation can be turned around and pivoted toward success.

We're all human.

We all face major and minor challenges. We all make mistakes and screw up sometimes.

What's important is how you react to those challenges and mistakes and how resilient you are.

I have used my previous mistakes as a learning process, and I am going to help you avoid, or at least be prepared for, all the pitfalls that can occur on the long road to success.

That is why I developed my unique DREAM self-improvement program.

I used this system to achieve my dreams and now I am sharing it with you so you can use my DREAM to achieve yours.

It is an easy formula to remember and to practice. You can make it part of your everyday routine.

But please remember that training your brain to operate at its full potential is the same as training your body.

My DREAM system is not a six or 12-week course you can dip in and out of.

It takes discipline and application over a sustained period of time.

You need to live the DREAM every minute of every day.

What you learn from the book needs to be applied in every aspect of your life.

You never know when you are going to need to be prepared for challenge.

You must accept the fact that you are going to grow and change into a more successful version of yourself, and that can be a painful process.

But you will emerge the other side feeling happier and more prosperous than you have ever felt.

My simple learning is this – the amount of reward that you receive is directly linked to the amount of effort you put in.

This applies to everything in your life from personal relationships to career success.

If you want to be exceptional, then you must be prepared to work and hustle harder than everyone else.

If you want to be 100 times more successful than the average person, then you must put in 100 times more effort than the average person.

It is a straightforward equation but a challenging thing to achieve.

Fearless means not giving in or running away from challenges or threats – real and imagined.

It means being confident, brave and bold in thought and action.

Most importantly, to make something or someone fearless requires preparation so that resilience can be developed in advance of the challenge.

I promise you - the only thing stopping you from fulfilling your dreams is you.

Let me help you change that.

My DREAM system is going to be your guide to help you deliver the best version of yourself every day for optimum results and a life-changing transformation.

Prepare to dream to achieve.

Prepare to become fearless!

DREAM

Chapter 1: Determination

I am so grateful to have been born and brought up in Belfast in the 1970s and 80s.

Why?

Because my home city is tangible proof that impossible transformation can happen.

But it only happened because the right mindset and actions made it work by people determined to succeed.

Northern Ireland had to believe there was no such thing as impossible if it was going to get beyond its troubled past.

By the time you finish reading this book, you will be achieving the 'impossible' for yourself as I guide you through my Five Golden Principles of Dream to Achieve.

Belfast is inspirational because of how quickly it transformed from being a failure to an incredible city to be proud of.

When you realise in the last 20 years Belfast has transformed from a place of bombs, bullets and bad business, to being voted as one the top cities in the world for tourism, you can see why I am justifiably proud of its resilience and determination.

Growing up against the backdrop of constant political violence, I couldn't even imagine a different future for myself or the city.

We had to challenge how things had been done in the past and find new strategies.

But plans are nothing without action, (remember that as we go through this book!).

Hard work, resilience, fearlessness, commitment, self-sacrifice, dedication, leadership and particularly determination was required from both sides of a bitterly divide society to deliver change in Belfast.

With vision and collective determination, after 40 years of conflict, Northern Ireland overwhelmingly voted for peace in 1998.

We achieved what everyone thought was impossible.

But we had to believe a better future was possible; then we had to commit to working hard to achieve it.

And that's not the end of the story because success is not a one-off event.

You need to consistently and determinedly work at, (remember that as well!)

In fact, there are still countless unsung heroes, from community leaders to politicians, on the ground in Northern Ireland working hard every day to maintain peace.

So, suppose you want to make the impossible possible in your life.

You need to employ the same tactics Belfast used to achieve its incredible transformation from wrecked-house to power-house.

You must believe, commit, act, then continually work to maintain and improve.

Now you get an insight into why this city gave me my unbreakable determination to achieve my full potential.

I wanted – No – I needed to be part of Belfast's ongoing success story.

I wanted to contribute to this proud city's story myself.

It now fills me with immense pride that my successful businesses genuinely improve life in the city. I'm paying my dues to my hometown and Belfast keeps repaying my faith in its determination to succeed against the odds.

As a native of Belfast, I know its potential, its unbreakable resilience in the face of adversity. I aspire to match its spirit. Belfast is a fighter, and I always knew it could pull itself off the ropes. So, 20 years ago, when the city came back swinging, I was already in its corner.

Even before I established Dream Luxury Serviced Apartments in June 2017, I was already looking well ahead.

I wanted to spot opportunities coming down the track before anyone else could even imagine such potential. It's a skill I developed at an early age, and it has served me well.

But vision and belief are useless unless you have the determination to act.

So I planned and invested my faith and capital and believed that the Universe, (and my city), would deliver dividends. And they both did.

But don't think success comes without hard work. What makes the difference between being mediocre and being exceptional is the core determination to be the best you can be.

This can only be achieved by the drive to work above and beyond even what you think you are capable of and the willingness to strive to take the extreme actions required to excel.

Personal fulfilment is not a destination – it's a journey.

It's a process that needs to be continuously renewed and reviewed.

It needs the energy to progress, and that energy only comes from within.

You must develop the inner resilience to keep pushing even when it seems too challenging to go on.

Let me explain to you why determination is so important. It comes number one on my list because it is the baseline for everything else we are going to explore and pursue.

Determination is the quality that you show when you have decided to do something, and you will not let anything stop you.

It's about having the ability to continue trying even when it's difficult.

Determination is the key to all human success.

Trust me; a dream doesn't become a reality through some kind of magic process.

It takes commitment, hard work and mostly determination.

Some people are content to simply dream of success while others wake up, dress up, show up and work hard at it.

Determination is the driving force which turns any dream into a reality.

First and foremost, self-belief is the core of determination.

It's important to remember that those who have mastered determination are not necessarily people who have never failed.

However, the difference is that they get back up and keep going and learn from what went wrong.

They change their behaviour, form a new plan and believe in themselves, despite monumental setbacks. They don't take no for an answer.

They are determined to always turn 'No' into 'Yes', no matter what it costs. Exceptional people are an unstoppable force.

They are an unmovable object.

And are unapologetic about it.

They never give up at the first challenge and will persist in their goals with more determination than anyone else. It's this ability to keep getting up and finding new solutions is what delivers fulfilment.

This is the most crucial lesson my city taught me.

And it is just one core lesson I am going to teach you in this book.

I grew up in the 1970s in a suburb of Belfast located just nine miles from the very heart of the city. I have a brother and sister, and my parents set a great example when we were young and impressionable.

Life was fun and exciting for my siblings and me, but we respected our parents' law.

I was often in awe of my dad's quiet determination to get on with his job as a postman, despite the unusual and often violent backdrop of our everyday existence. The community depended on him to turn up with their mail every day - regardless of the challenges. And he did with pride and grace. Always stoic and calm, his life lesson to me was one of consistency and commitment.

My mother is fearless. She had to be as she was bringing up a young family against the backdrop of violent conflict in the 1970s and 80s. Thankfully, she taught me that same quality, and I bring that into every thought I have and every action I take – personal and professional.

My unique DREAM system for achievement needs you to cultivate that same mentality.

You need to be fearless so you can push yourself above and beyond everyone else.

You must be equally determined to push yourself beyond what you think you are capable of.

That takes some guts. But I've learned that to be exceptional you just can't be like everyone else.

You must be fearless and willing to step up to the challenge when no one else will and be willing to set the bar so high it is beyond the reach of everyone else.

The philosopher Arthur Schopenhauer once said – **'Talent hits a target no one else can hit, but genius hits a target no one else can see.'**

Here's my advice – develop the traits of a genius now. Believe there is a target beyond what you can actually see and aim for that.

Many people make a fundamental mistake in setting their goals far too small.

You will, of course, meet obstacles and suffer disappointments so you should set your aim higher than what you currently believe is necessary.

Challenge the preconceptions that have put boundaries around your ambitions.

Do you realise these limitations have been set for you without your consent through education, upbringing and social class?

All factors outside your control.

They are making you underestimate your potential and your abilities.

Do you want to play by someone else's rules?

Rules made to create an uneven playing field where the low expectations of others burden you.

If you are happy with that, then give up now or follow my advice and write your own rules to benefit you.

Who is going to stop you?

Your story starts in your mind and is supported through by your actions.

My advice is to set what others believe are 'unrealistic goals' – in other words, aim always to take the Gold Medal.

So even if you fall short in your ultimate goal, you will still be on the winners' podium.

If you aim for the Bronze medal and fail, then you will miss all glory, success and recognition.

But suppose you are already up on those winners' steps. In that case, it's much easier to move from Bronze to Silver to Gold the next time by utilising small improvements and increased insight and knowledge.

Nobody remembers the person who comes second.

You can spend your time realising your own goals, or other people will simply use you to achieve their dreams.

If you set small targets, it stands to reason that you will just get small wins.

With limited vision comes limited action, and you won't invest the appropriate time or effort into getting what you really want because you are so distracted by unambitious goals.

You just won't have the necessary resources in place to overcome the inevitable challenges in your quest.

I don't need to tell you that the world recognises and rewards excellence.

Take the example of an elite athlete. To achieve the very top levels of success in their chosen sport, first and foremost, they need to believe they can win that Olympic Gold Medal.

Then they need the determination to train hard every day, regardless of the challenges.

They are rewarded for dedication and sacrifice over many years of their lives by being recognised as a winner.

You know, there are probably better natural swimmers, runners and players out in the world.

But what distinguishes winners is that they harness their abilities and focus them to fulfil their potential.

Winners are prepared to whatever it takes to succeed.

They set the highest targets, take decisive action and remain committed every minute of every day to their objectives.

In the race of life, wouldn't you rather be an elite athlete, rather than a plodder in the pack?

But think about it, if a player has no target to shoot for then how they will score a goal?

It really helps to visualise what you want and keep those real images in front of you to motivate your every action.

If you can dream it, you can achieve it. If you can see it, you will achieve it quicker.

I do this by creating a vision board which hangs on the wall right in front of my desk.

I put pictures of the things I want to achieve to inspire and remind me what precisely I'm working towards.

Visualisation or dream boards are so simple to create that you can make one right now.

It will prove the most valuable visualisation tool available to you, and it is basically free and fun to make.

HOW TO MAKE TOM'S DREAM BOARD

- A Dream Board is a special gift to yourself so make sure you set aside time to really focus and think about it. A dream board is an amazing reminder of what you truly want in life and a powerful motivator to enact on achieving your goals.
- Refuse to place limits on yourself as you construct your vision board! Keep it positive and motivating.
- Plan your board carefully – take time to think exactly what you want. Consider the following: What are your values? What are your career targets? Are you happy with your family or love life? What are your expectation in terms of your health and your wealth? What do you want to become?
- Choosing the right images to stimulate your actions is important. Select pictures, quotes or even images of your heroes from magazines or online. These images should mirror your desires and you need to feel a strong connection to them to stimulate your thoughts and actions. Remember that your subconscious mind responds to pictures and images that trigger an emotional reaction. Each picture on your vision board should therefore produce a positive emotional reaction when you look at it.
- Your board should reflect your personality and style and be attractive to look at.
- Once you create your dream board, display it in a place where you can see it every day. Take the time to reflect on your targets. Your dream board needs to charge you with renewed passion whenever you look at it. Over time, as you move closer toward your desired future, some of the images may not make as much of an emotional impression. When you notice this, update your vision board with fresh images to inspire you.
- Your dream board should always be a work in progress. It needs to be a dynamic mirror of your targets that changes as your dreams and desires change.

These inspirational collages are the images of your future and show a tangible example, idea or representation of the targets you are aiming for.

They should represent your dreams, your goals, and your ideal life. They are powerful and effective tools which will help you narrow down your desires and help give you laser-like focus.

Science has proved that the human mind responds more quickly and effectively to visual stimulations. So the best way to achieve your goals is to keep them in the front of your mind, so you're always looking for ways to move closer to them.

A vision board will act as a constant reminder of why you are doing what you are doing. When you see something that inspires you every day, you stay on track.

Even when you face setbacks, that vision board will still be there ready to motivate you all over again. It will help you passionately connect with your goals.

In my experience, when you are fired up and passionate, you are much more likely to take the appropriate action to get what you want.

By putting a vision board where you can see it every day, you will prompt yourself to visualise your targets more clearly.

This visualisation will activate the creative powers of your subconscious mind.

It will program your brain to notice available opportunities that will move you closer to your goals.

A vision board will help you clarify what you really want. In the process of creating this board, you will be forced to sit and consider what you want from your life.

It will also help you think differently and re-prioritise your goals and actions.

Our brain is geared toward making us successful with every action we take. It trains our bodies to prepare for action. Hence, when you imagine preparing for an activity, your brain is way ahead rehearsing the process and send out signals to the rest of your body to complete the action.

A study looking at weightlifters' brains revealed the patterns activated when they lifted hundreds of pounds were similarly activated when they only imagined lifting.

This clearly shows mind practice is almost as effective as physical training, and that combining both is much more effective than either alone.

It's been found that mental exercises can enhance motivation, increase confidence and self-reliance and improves performance - all-important when you are determined to achieve your best life! So prime your brain first for success.

There is a power in what you fix your eyes on.

A vision board enables you to focus your view on your goals to make them your reality. What's in your mind will determine the types of decisions you make.

This is what makes a vision board such a valuable tool for aiming your focus in the direction of your dreams. You should display pictures of how you want your future life to be.

Being able to actually see what your conscious mind desires will help your subconscious mind to go to work on your behalf to make it possible.

It also helps your brain's information filtering system, (the reticular activating system (RAS)), tune into the opportunities that will move you closer to that desired reality.

Remarkably, visualisation is nearly as powerful as performing the action itself.

So when you visualise yourself living in your dream home, your brain trains your body for that reality.

You are ready to seize the opportunity and mold the world to your desires.

For example, and this is a true story from my life, I saw a beautiful house for sale that I fell in love with and wanted to buy.

So I put a photo of the house on my vision board. Unfortunately, this particular house had already just been sold to another person.

Undeterred, I knew I was going to buy and live in that house, so the picture took the centre spot on my dream board.

Two weeks after being told it was sold, the real estate agent phoned me back to say the sale had fallen through and I could have it. He was stunned when I confidently replied 'of course it did, I told you I was going to buy that house.'

I believed, and the Universe repaid my faith and hard work. I still live in my dream house today.

However, don't think merely wishing for something makes it materialise, unless of course you have a magic lamp and even then you only get three wishes! (I will come back to this story later in the book).

Of course, you have to dream big to achieve big. But remember, the end goal in itself is not that important.

Whether you want to lose weight, earn a million pound a year or be the best in your profession, you are going to need to move and change your mindset with tremendous determination.

Research has revealed that just focusing on attaining your goal, as opposed to thinking about the effort it will take to succeed, will increase your chances of failure.

Think about it – everyone has dreams to be a top athlete, movie star, bestselling author, etc.

The real challenge is not determining if you want the result, but if you are willing to accept the sacrifices required to achieve your goal.

Goals are useful for pointing to the right direction. But action is needed to actually make progress.

So writing down your goals is like putting the co-ordinates of your destination into a Sat Nav but you still have to make the journey to get there and that takes effort.

Exceptional success cannot be achieved by anything less than exceptional vision and targeted actions. Remember, it stands to reason that average efforts deliver average results.

And average success is no success.

Given a choice, would you rather be average or exceptional?

Which do you believe returns the most significant personal satisfaction and results?

Trust me; if you start any project or action without expanding your vision and setting your targets above what others believe is achievable, then you are limiting your outcomes before you even begin.

You are unwittingly self-sabotaging your potential, and this will have a knock-on effect on your actions. In other words, the script you write for yourself will be the outcome you get.

You have a choice. You can waste time energy and resources merely competing with yourself or other people, or you can be the apex predator at the top of the food chain. Both require the same amount of input; however, the more successful person has the determination to be at the top.

This position of market superiority and personal discipline brings with it resilience and self-belief.

Do you successfully complete a journey in your car by looking in the rear-view mirror at the traffic behind you?

No, of course not.

You get out your map and plot the journey, and then you look forward in the direction you want to travel.

You overtake to get there quicker and look ahead to see the gaps you can utilise to advance your mission.

The minute you lose focus or take your eyes off what's ahead, then you are going to crash and burn.

Many brilliantly-talented, creative and intelligent people never reach their potential because of lack of direction.

You always need a clear plan to get you from A to B.

You can have the most expensive car in the world, still, if you set off without a clear idea of where you're going, then someone in a rusty old banger with determination, a compass and a map will beat you every time.

You must be so consumed and focused on your personal goals as not to become distracted in other people's power plays.

It's your game, so you set the rules, and only you know what personal success feels like.

Only you know the exact definition of what you need to do or whom you need to be to feel successful.

But it is important to remember that success is not just a fleeting moment.

You always need to work to keep, maintain and build on your concept of success.

You must define what you must do to keep adding to your definition of success.

Focus on the exceptional and never limit your vision or your target. Compromise is expensive, and you always pick up the tab.

You need to be the bullet, not the target. You are the only person who can make this happen.

What drove me to my current level of success is the sheer determination to control my own destiny.

As I said, I cultivated the ability to look ahead and plan for the future early in my life.

I started early, but you can start anytime. Now is always the best time to make yourself better.

At 10-years-old, I persuaded my friend's older sister to get me a job in the local fast food joint.

I started on the very bottom rung of the career ladder as the lad who peeled the potatoes to make fries. It was so cold that I had to stand in a bucket of warm water in my bare feet to keep the circulation going.

As you can imagine, the pay was pitiful. But it was money I didn't have and, regardless of the amount, it was my primary motivation to go to work.

I didn't do it because I enjoyed standing in the cold peeling potatoes for hours on end. No, I did it because it was a means to an end. It was the golden key to my self-esteem and status.

I envisioned my end goal, and I was determined to achieve it. I learned that no matter how difficult or how painful the process, you must be determined to keep going until you reach what you want.

Then you have to keep going to maintain and build on that success.

When you are exhausted, keep going and never stop.

I worked in that chip shop for five years because I was determined to achieve my ultimate goal.

It taught me tough but valuable lessons. I was determined to earn my own money, so I could buy the latest fashions my friends all had. I learned that if I wanted to be respected, I had to work to achieve that respect.

This was my core motivation, and it drove me to go to my job and endure extreme conditions.

I admit it seemed harsh at the time I had to work so hard to buy the latest trends when all my teenage mates just tapped up their parents.

But my mum and dad didn't believe in getting into debt. If you couldn't afford it, you didn't get it.

Simple.

What I realise now was my parents set a great baseline rule which I still apply today. If you want to own something, you have to be prepared to work hard to get it.

Like my trendy teenage fashion shopping, the drive was about much more than merely buying clothes. It was about boosting self-esteem with the outward display of the rewards of my hard work.

It is the best feeling in the world! I still get the same sense of pride today when I do a deal or achieve something I desire as I did spending my wages from the chip shop on a new shirt when I was a kid.

That proves to me how fundamental it is to be genuinely motivated to achieve your goals.

Having such insight into the motivating psychology of precisely what drives purchases would come in useful in my first proper job as manager of a sports clothing shop.

This is where I got my first taste of proper success. I was a natural salesman and quickly realised by developing this talent, I would be rewarded. If anyone tells you sales is difficult, then they are a failed salesperson!

With such an attitude, they cannot and will not ever succeed.

I set myself 'impossible targets', and I achieved them and won a reputation and financial bonuses for having the best sales in the national group. I wanted the achievement, the recognition and the reward, and I worked hard to make sure I attained these goals.

After completing my studies at high school, I attended a technical college to study Leisure Management. My mum had instilled in me, that I always needed an education to fall back on.

Subsequently, I have learned that an education isn't only delivered in school.

Every day is an education as the world is continuously in flux. You need to be flexible and resilient enough to adapt to change and harness it for your own purposes.

I realised the value and security of owning bricks and mortar and in 1993, aged just, 19 I bought my first house.

Because of the violent political situation and reduced wages, house prices in Northern Ireland before the ceasefire were notoriously low, so this proved to be an excellent investment at just the right time. I trusted the Universe to deliver, made a plan and determinedly worked hard at it to make my dream a reality.

I ignored the challenges of my location and the rejected the idea that I couldn't do it because I came from a working class background.

But, I was smart enough to realise that there is no such thing as an overnight success.

I also learned early in my career that people will only recognise success when they see it.

They don't see or acknowledge the hard work that goes into it, making it happen.

Like most worthless things in life, talk is cheap and action costs. The price is hard work and determination.

I instinctively knew I had to establish a firm base to build on, and my modest first property was to be it.

My life had been set on a new trajectory because I had the vision and drive at an early age to do something different.

I decided to rewrite the script of failure that was predestined to me.

And you can do the same with the right mental tools and life skills, which I am going to share based on my own life experiences. My fortunes and those of Belfast dramatically changed in ways that once seemed impossible and so can yours. You just need the determination to transform your life for unlimited success.

And I am going to reveal to you the secrets of just how to do that through my unique DREAM system.

Mission Statement

Success is not a destination – it's a journey.

You are the only person who can make this happen.

TOM'S TIPS TO DEVELOP DETERMINATION

- Determination is the driving force which turns any dream into a reality. Be determined to be exceptional in everything you do.
- Now is always the best time to make yourself better.
- Never take 'No' for an answer.
- Be Fearless.
- Don't limit your potential by setting your targets too low.
- Average action delivers average results. And average success is no success.
- Have defined goals and stick to your plan to achieve them.
- To be exceptional you must be prepared to work above and beyond even what you think you are capable of.
- Don't be distracted in other people's power plays. Always aim to be the apex in your sector.
- No matter how difficult or how painful the process you must be determined to keep going until you achieve what you want.

DREAM

Chapter 2: Regeneration

I am genuinely grateful that I have the power to reinvent and regenerate myself every day.

Regeneration is the key to basic survival, whether you are an animal, human being or even a city.

You may not realise it, but your body is regenerating all day, every day to ensure you stay physically healthy.

Cells rebuild and renew themselves every moment, and much of our bodies are renewed every three to four weeks.

Just think you are a whole new you in only one month without having to do anything!

Imagine what you could achieve in terms of positive change if you really work at it in a conscious and well-planned way.

You can trust your body and the Universe to just get on with constant regeneration.

But accelerated mental and psychological renewal needs decisions and actions from you.

Your cells may change by themselves, but your thoughts don't so you require active practice to change your mindset.

And my DREAM system is going to help you supercharge your attitude and continuously renew your positivity.

Albert Einstein said: **'We cannot solve our problems with the same level of thinking that created them.'**

So you must shake yourself out of your comfort zone and raise your level of thinking to the exceptional.

Don't be put off if you have experienced, (or are experiencing,) failure – no matter how major.

Even in the most extreme crisis, like the world's economy being shut down, (which is happening as I write this right now!), there are opportunities.

But you will only find them if you have the right mindset and attitude to succeed.

So when the COVID-19 pandemic hit unexpectedly in March 2020, I employed my self-belief and positive mindset to power through the crisis.

All my drive, actions and thoughts were being motivated by my inner reserves because there was little positive external input.

Like an athlete facing their greatest sporting challenge, I recognised that I had to up my game.

I told my body and mind to take it up a gear and move out of the comfort zone.

I was going out to do battle with the most significant economic crisis faced by humanity since the Second World War but I knew I would survive and flourish.

And guess what – I proved my DREAM system is effective even in the greatest global crisis faced by humanity in decades.

I was able to EXPAND my business while everyone else around me was crumbling.

I did this not by waiting on opportunities to come my way, but by getting out there and creating them myself.

While almost everyone else hid in their bunkers waiting for the storm to pass, I was out there using the power of the storm to propel my ambitions.

Remember – planes take off against the wind, not with it.

You need a jet engine behind your thoughts and actions to gain altitude.

When the world was frightened and uncertain, I was out there making things happen and reaping the benefits of less competition and an unstable marketplace.

I was fearless, so of course, I succeeded over the fearful.

It makes sense, right?

To paraphrase Rudyard Kipling's famous poem – **'If you can keep your head when all about you are losing theirs, yours is the earth and everything that's in it.'**

So follow my lead and don't wait for your ship to come in – swim out like a pirate king and take over the boat you want, which is laden with the most treasure!

Remember, whatever you imagine yourself to be, that's what you will become.

So envisage yourself as a winner and a warrior.

Keep the company of successful and positive people who build you up and recharge your batteries. Find people who can create opportunities and connections for you.

Stay away from losers who drain your energy and drag you into their zone of negativity.

You know the saying about dress for the job you want, not the job you have?

The same applies to your mindset.

It is my mindset that has carried me through the 2020 pandemic crisis.

But trust me – mindset is not something you are just born with.

You need to work at every day in the same way a dedicated elite athlete trains to compete.

Every day in life is a competition, so you need always to be mentally fit if you want to be on the winners' podium each time.

I achieved success in the face of extreme challenges because I have the same attitude as a raging bull!

I'm unashamedly going to keep going forward to achieve all of my ambitious goals.

I will destroy all obstacles that get in the way.

I will smash any negativity that drains my positivity.

If you want success, you need to think and act the same way as me.

You need a single-minded vision that you are not prepared to compromise on.

When things are tough, that's when you need to be able to step up.

Don't judge a person on how they behave when everything is going well.

Judge them by how they respond when the journey to success gets really, really hard - which it inevitably will.

That's when most people will simply give up and stay on the mediocre level.

This is the very reason why not everyone can experience real success in life because not everyone can overcome those challenges.

With my DREAM system, I am giving you the mental tools to take you right to the summit of success.

Still, you need to take responsibility to use them properly and practice every day.

Success is not a destination, it's a journey.

If you want to be exceptional and live your DREAM, then you need to keep believing that nothing can stop you from achieving your goals.

NOTHING.

I have learned only maximum effort will deliver the ultimate rewards.

So if you thought you were working hard before when you were making 20 sales calls, now you must complete 200 calls instead.

Up your effort to increase your reward.

That's the only way you will get exceptional results.

That's the only way to be fearless in business.

RISE OR FALL?   IT'S YOUR CALL!

Let me share with you my experience of a significant renewal in my life.

I once suffered a considerable business setback resulting in substantial financial loss.

In retrospect, I realised this happened because I did not do my due diligence properly.

I wavered and didn't follow my own advice. A hard lesson was learned well.

At this point, I had two options.

Give up and get stuck in the rut of failure or change gear and work 100 times harder not just to get back to where I was before, but actually to exceed it.

I chose the latter option, but I had to literally regenerate myself, my personal life, my professional life – in fact, everything about myself.

I took responsibility for the situation and assessed where I had gone wrong.

The only resources I had available to me were what was inside my mind.

My attitude was the only tool I had left to dig myself out of a very deep hole.

I looked again to Belfast and its ability to regenerate for success, and I was inspired to match it.

I realised one failure wouldn't determine my destiny.

But this can only be achieved by employing vision, ambition and massive actions.

I have learned that persistence cannot be beaten, regardless of the challenges.

You need to cultivate personal discipline and full commitment and be obsessed with your goals.

Then translate this energy in to action to make it happen.

To be exceptional and achieve your dreams, you must always be prepared to go further than everyone else to get what you want.

We will touch again on this idea of going to extremes to get the job done later and I will reveal my WIT system in much greater detail in my next book to be published soon entitled **Whatever It Takes.**

EMBRACE CHANGE & LET GO

Continual change is both inevitable and necessary.

Don't try to swim against the tide. Instead, learn to use the energy of renewal to move you towards your goals.

I have faced significant challenges, but I bounced back.

The only reason I could pull myself back up from rock bottom is because I believed I could do it.

I told myself I could overcome adversity and flourish.

Against the odds, I built myself back up, and I'm now a significant player in Belfast's leisure sector. Through my hospitality and property companies, I am currently contributing to the city's international success.

I believed I could turn things around and enjoy a better future, and so did Belfast.

Our partnership is the perfect powerhouse of positivity.

I was able to harness Belfast's unexpected renewal to help me build my hugely successful businesses.

My city's rejuvenation has been beneficial to me, but only because I anticipated and embraced developments in Belfast's culture, global status and architecture.

Now, I'm helping drive the city's world-class ambitions by providing quality and affordable short-stay accommodation for tourists and the business sector.

Proof that success breeds success and that self-belief can move mountains.

Look to the future because that's the only thing you have the power to change.

Always remember, what has past is gone.

All past mistakes and successes are over; their energy is spent.

You need to set down all the heavy, pointless baggage of regret, pride and guilt.

I learned this lesson in a very real way during an intense training session with Daniel Konieczny, my business coach.

He asked me to hold up the light briefcase I was carrying.

After a minute or so, he enquired if I thought it was heavy.

I replied "no, of course not."

After five minutes, he asked me the same question, and I had to admit the bag was beginning to feel heavier than when I first started holding it.

37

Then Daniel asked to visualise how it would feel holding that bag up for an hour, then a day, a week, a month and then a year.

He wanted to make the point that emotional baggage gathers more weight the longer you hold on to it.

The more you to cling to it, the heavier it becomes as your strength diminishes.

You need to set it down and let it go.

Only take the learning experience forward.

If you live in the past, you take your eye off the ball in the present.

That's how you miss future opportunities.

Continually looking back on past mistakes or previous triumphs means you fail to create your future self which takes constant work, training and input.

The past is called the past for a reason – it's gone.

Pioneering American industrialist Henry Ford said: **'Whether you think you can, or you think you can't - you're right.'**

This quote means that people's beliefs about their abilities directly determines if they will succeed or fail at a task, or even life.

Our beliefs about our capabilities are essential because believing you will enjoy success increases your chances of having actual success.

While judging yourself as not capable of achieving success reduces your chances of succeeding.

The power of your mind literally determines the outcomes of your actions.

What you believe about yourself is the energy you project out into the world, and it's what will rebound back to you.

I would define this as your attitude, and your attitude is a crucial determinant of your success.

So here's my advice - get an exceptional attitude to life right now if you want to achieve extraordinary results.

And more wisdom from Henry Ford: **'One of the greatest discoveries a person makes, one of their great surprises, is to find they can do what they were afraid they couldn't do.'**

I want to illustrate self-belief and regeneration with a story about a personal friend of mine which epitomises Ford's wisdom about challenging yourself and pushing through the fear of failure.

In June 2017, Belfast boxer Ryan Burnett was crowned unified bantamweight world champion, having held the WBA (Unified) and IBF titles between 2017 and 2018.

Indeed, an incredible achievement.

Even more so when you realise that just three years before lifting the world title, Ryan was was staring into the abyss of failure through circumstances beyond his control.

Through no fault of his own, he was so close to losing everything he had worked so hard to achieve.

After battling career-threatening health issues and going through a split with his high-profile manager, Ryan had just about lost everything - except his fighting spirit.

Ryan Burnett was so determined to be a winner and a champion, that he was prepared to live in a car for six weeks just so he could continue training.

After losing his management contract, Ryan and his father struggled to find accommodation in England and ended up sleeping in a borrowed car while waiting on a confirmation of a new manager.

Ryan had enough self-belief, determination and talent to believe he was a winner.

He was prepared to do whatever was needed to achieve his dream.

Even if that meant that both he, and his ever-supportive father, had to suffer the deprivations of effectively making themselves homeless for six weeks.

Back in Belfast, Ryan's mum had a warm bed and hot meals waiting at home but he rejected his comfort zone and pushed himself beyond the limits of human endurance both inside and outside of the ring.

He didn't just throw in the towel – even in the face of incredible adversity.

He had dreamt since childhood of becoming a world champion.

He had promised his mother and father he would become world champion.

And he faced every adversity in his path like a world champion.

Then he became the world champion.

Then Double World Champion!

This amazingly positive attitude is what gave Ryan the inner reserves to reinvent and regenerate himself and succeed against the odds.

Ryan was never afraid to do what he knew he could do.

He is a true hero.

Ryan Burnett went from facing extreme personal and professional challenges to becoming world champion in three years because he believed he could.

There's the real inspiration for you to copy!

If you want to be a champion, you have to think, train and fight like a champion every single day.

Does your life feel like the movie 'Groundhog Day' where nothing changes day after day?

Well, that's because you are allowing it to be like that.

Have you forgotten you're the scriptwriter of the blockbuster of your life?

So why are you giving yourself a crappy story?

When you need motivation, just remember Ryan Burnett and cast yourself as a boxing hero like Rocky Balboa.

Aspire to be a world champion in your career and recognise that you must work exceptionally hard to make it happen.

REJECT ALL LIMITATIONS

If you want to be exceptional, you need to take exceptional actions.

Be aware that sometimes means your efforts will seem unreasonable to others.

Honestly, that's what is needed for success – especially when it comes to sales.

Set aside preconceived notions of how things are done and find new and more productive ways to improve your life.

Challenge everything like a fearless warrior as weak people are simply happy to coast along.

They won't challenge the status quo because it might involve more effort they don't want to use.

Laziness means loss of control and submission to just being mediocre.

Exceptional people are mentally and physically strong and are prepared to work hard to maintain their advantages.

They are tough enough to challenge and to rebel. They are strong enough to be unreasonable.

Irish writer George Bernard Shaw said: **'All progress is made by unreasonable people because reasonable people adjust to their surroundings and unreasonable people rebel against their surroundings and produce progress.'**

So stop being reasonable!

Being unreasonable means not accepting any limitations.

It means doing things that everyone thinks are too much or not logical.

It means doing things that are easy to dream but seem impossible to achieve.

Progress never happens in a reasonable, comfortable, or safe place.

So be unreasonable because your success depends on it.

Being unreasonable means you have no reasons to prevent your progress.

An unreasonable person takes action rather than making excuses.

When you become unreasonable, you find ways to do what you want to do right now.

When you are unreasonable, you choose to act in the present moment—without a need for reasons.

Stop focusing on why you can't do something and, instead, focus on why you can.

Remember, all change or forward movement happens in the instant you choose something different and take a step into that decision.

If you want to be exceptional, you need to regenerate your thoughts and trust your intuition, act quickly, and stop looking for reasons not to do something.

This is the only way to achieve the impossible.

Why?

Because the so-called impossible couldn't happen in somebody else's script.

So successful people ignore that limiting script and they write their own.

They reject 'the logical' and 'the reasonable' because it is not delivering what they really want to achieve.

Always remember 'the rules' of the game have been set by someone else, so they hold the advantage.

If you want that advantage, you need to ignore how things are done by others and do it your way.

Set your own rules and play the game your way.

BE A GIANT DISRUPTOR

Be a confident disruptor because your vision is unique, and you can see the solutions others can't.

That's why people like Bill Gates, Steve Jobs and Elon Musk are giants in their field.

They ignored what everyone else said was impossible.

They set their sights beyond the target and embraced the mindset of the exceptional.

They delivered world-changing products which made them hugely successful.

There is a recognisable pattern of success here.

Believe in yourself, identify your goals, take massive actions and just get shit done!

Believe me; your competitors are not going to come and offer you the opportunity to take them on by doing something different.

Why would they?

Their success depends on you believing that just because things have always been done a certain way, that's the right and only way to do it.

You are playing by your competitors' rules without even realising it.

Be prepared to set and play by your own rules - be a wolf, not a sheep.

Break out of the general flock of humanity where 'sheep' mentality inhibits your unique thoughts.

Be a predator always hunting for opportunities and creating advantages to take the prize.

Be at the head of the table, not on the menu.

The wolf never waits to be invited to dinner.

Look to the top level in the chain of command and challenge the status quo until you get there.

Don't stop until you become the apex predator at the top of the food chain.

And keep challenging it even when you think you have reached the pinnacle.

I learned this lesson when I brought high-quality, self-serviced apartments to Belfast for the first time when the city's accommodation sector was based almost entirely on hotels.

The established industry thought I was mad.

The official tourist organisations were anxious about change.

Everyone tried their hardest to convince me that my Dream Luxury Serviced Apartments plan wouldn't work.

The naysayers were not worried about helping me.

They just wanted to protect their own interests and keep the game the same because it suited them.

Change and regeneration were not on their agenda.

They were happy to rest on previous success.

They didn't change, but the market did as consumer requirements adapted to the online world.

And I was ready.

If I had been reasonable and applied their logic, I wouldn't have pushed ahead with my plans.

They would have less competition, and I wouldn't have success.

That would be good for them - but bad for me.

Believe me, when I say, I am not in the business of creating wealth and success for other people.

I was open to new ideas when I saw the success of serviced apartments in other cities in the world because I wasn't locked into the conventional way of thinking.

I always embrace renewal and change because I know they bring opportunities.

So I looked ahead to a world of independent travellers who would be proactively booking online.

They want affordable, good quality accommodation where they could set their own agenda.

I recognised that the needs of the modern traveller had changed.

Hence, I delivered a modern solution that my business competitors didn't even see coming.

I could be described as unreasonable because I ignored the established logic, but it has proved a winning strategy.

In just five years, I went from opening to completely dominating the local market and expanding my business interest internationally.

I became the Wolf of Belfast.

INVENT YOUR OWN FUTURE

Let me share a secret with you – all successful people love change and renewal.

They embrace it and are always ready to exploit it to their advantage.

They anticipate change.

With the 2020 global pandemic and the chaotic markets following in its wake, you need to be ready to face any challenge.

There's no time to feel sorry for yourself.

You must do what you need to do, not just to survive, but also flourish.

It's that mindset that has allowed my Dream concept to emerge from this crisis as number one in the sector.

I have found the most accurate way to predict the future is to invent it.

This means getting ahead of inevitable change.

An upset in the status quo can deliver dividends, but only if you are prepared to grab them.

Everything is changing all the time.

Naturally, when things are working well, you don't want to change them.

Still, as an exceptional person committed to being a winner, you should always be looking to improve.

That means looking forward and anticipating the change to harness it, rather than simply being overwhelmed or bypassing it.

This is what you need to do to be a champion.

You must always look ahead, seek potential and make calculated decisions based on the acceptance of inevitable change.

In my experience, it's better to make continual adjustments, rather than to do nothing, then try to figure out what went wrong.

By then you generally need to make significant and often expensive changes to fix it.

POSITIVE SELF IMPROVEMENT

Change and renewal are the twin engines of innovation because people get bored quickly and lose interest in the familiar.

'New and Improved' are brilliant words for attracting consumer attention, and that's why they appear so much in advertisements.

You must apply the same theory to your thoughts and actions if you want to achieve your ambitions.

Think about it – the biggest, most successful and instantly recognisable brands in the world are built on improvement, change and renewal.

For example, Apple releases new models and upgrades all the time because innovation and change drive sales and consumers don't want to be left behind.

McDonald's adds and changes its menu every few weeks for the same reason.

Car brands are always marketing upgraded models.

These mega-brands create their own opportunities for change.

So you can see how fundamental renewal and regeneration are to personal and professional success.

The good news is that you can upgrade and rejuvenate your personal brand with dedicated investment in yourself.

You can combine your physical training, (which I will discuss later in this chapter), with your mental stimulation by listening to audiobooks and podcasts as you work out in the gym or when you travel in the car.

Make your whole world a university of self-improvement and self-mentoring by listening to the wisdom and experience of others.

You can teach yourself to become an expert in anything through dedicated study.

But most importantly, you will learn to open your mind and free yourself of limiting thoughts.

This can be achieved through a change in mindset backed up by my unique Five Golden Principles of Dream to Achieve.

The 'power of positive thinking' is a well-used phrase, and sometimes it can feel a little clichéd.

But the physical and mental benefits of positive thinking have been clearly and repeatedly demonstrated in multiple independent scientific studies.

A positive mindset will give you more confidence, improve your mood and open your mind to the possibilities of regeneration.

You must fire up an incredibly positive mindset so you can convert every problem into a fixable challenge.

That way, you are never facing any obstacles to your success.

Your new mantra must be – 'There's no such thing as problems, merely challenges to be overcome.'

The more challenges you overcome, the more successful you will become.

Trust me, there's always another level for you to reach.

START YOUR DAY THE RIGHT WAY

You need to regenerate your thinking every day and the best time to do that is when you first wake up in the morning.

Personally, I now get up at 4am. I have found it to be the best time of the day.

I can do hours of mental and physical training before my working day even starts.

Honestly, how you start the morning sets the tone for the rest of the day.

Have you ever woken up late, been stressed and then felt like nothing good happened the rest of the day?

This is because you started the day with a negative emotion.

That pessimistic view carried into every other event you experienced and every decision you made.

You sent a negative attitude out, and the Universe responded to it with more negativity.

So be in control of your time and project the right script, so you get positive results.

Here's an example of what I mean.

I recently met an old friend and exchanged pleasantries, as you do.

He asked how I was doing, and I told him the truth. Life is excellent, the business is expanding, I'm flat out with opportunities, and I'm feeling fit and healthy.

His response to the same question was that he was just 'struggling on' and not having a great life.

I realised while chatting to him that he is continually putting out this negative and limiting script, and the Universe is just delivering what he is unwittingly ordering every day.

So change your words, and you will change your world.

Have a positive attitude from the moment you open your eyes every morning.

Say thank you the second your feet hit the floor. Always count your blessings before you count your money.

Instead of letting negativity dominate you, start your day with positive affirmations.

If you can't control your own thoughts, you won't be able to dictate their direction.

So don't start your day with a 'blocked channel' to the positivity that exists all around you.

You can regenerate your attitude daily with a healthy vision of yourself achieving the success you desire.

In this frame of mind, you are more likely to have a happier and healthier experience in everything you do, which opens the pathways for achievement.

Your energy is finite, so don't waste it on negativity.

For example, I hit the gym every morning without exception.

I don't give my mind permission to come up with any excuses to take the easy option and not do it.

I want to support, accelerate and harness my body's natural powers of regeneration to set me up in a positive frame of mind.

I want to supercharge my metabolism, so I have the energy to perform at my best all day.

I start my day at 4am with positivity and energy to set the tone for every thought and action.

I run through my goal statements as I complete my high-intensity cardio workout before hitting the gym at 7.30am.

My goal statements are my secret weapon, and as I am pounding on the running machine, I am shouting them all out repeatedly in my head.

I am operating at a level of high vibration. The Universe hears me because I'm calling out my goal statements with zero doubt that they are all going to happen.

When I hit the office at 8.45am, I have already spent almost four hours working on my physical, mental and spiritual resilience.

I have already achieved important goals before I start work, so I am radiating positive vibes that attract success.

I'm fully committed to this morning exercise regime because many studies have shown that it improves focus and mental ability and prepares me for ultimate performance. It also encourages discipline which carries over into many areas of my life.

Think about it – if you can create a healthy habit of morning regeneration based on physical exercise. Your metabolism will be flowing, you will look and feel better, your sleep will improve, and your mind will be sharper.

Exercise releases endorphins which are the body's natural happiness drug.

So, while it might not seem enjoyable to get out of the bed to exercise, you can be sure it's worth it.

You probably didn't pick up this book because you dream one day of becoming an Olympic athlete.

Therefore, you might be tempted to think you don't need to do physical exercise because you just want to improve your mental wellbeing.

But as your using my unique Five Golden Principles of Dream to Achieve to unleash the potential in your mind, you really need to extend it across your whole self to achieve maximum results.

There is no point having a high-performance engine in a car with lousy bodywork, is there?

You will never reach top speed because the drag factor of imperfection will always inhibit potential.

And so it is with your life so change it NOW!

There's little point being full of ambition and ideas if you don't have the physical energy, stamina and strength to get your plans done.

If you want to be exceptional, you can't be lazy in thought or action.

GET UP AND GET IT DONE

So even if you are not into extreme fitness, I recommend you set up a positive early morning routine underpinned by physical exercise to prepare yourself for the challenges of the day ahead.

A journey of a thousand miles starts with a single step, so even begin with a walk to clear your head, then build up your fitness regime by setting personal goals and targets.

Project forward and think about how you will feel as you smash those goals.

Trust me, in just 30 days of applied practice, like me, you will be a morning workout person, and you will start every day as a winner.

TOM'S TOP TIPS FOR REGENERATIVE DAILY EXERCISE

While it sounds like a difficult thing to achieve, let me share a few simple tips that will see you leaping out of bed and embracing your new fitness regime:

- Personal insight: Sounds obvious, but you need to think about why you are doing it.
- Don't do it because I have told you to do it – that won't work.
- You must be self-motivated as you will be the only person policing your actions.
- You need to have a solid, personally-compelling reason to get out of bed and get moving every morning.
- Nothing exceptional is ever easy, but it is worth the effort.
- Only you can decide how much time and effort you invest. But be assured, your effort will be reflected in the value of your returns.
- Remember – if you do what is easy, life is hard. If you do what is hard, life is easy.

JUST DO IT: Take action! Getting in shape isn't going to happen overnight. Following my DREAM system, it needs to be done continually and consistently to push for more exceptional results.

If you're just starting with exercise, don't do too much too soon.

This will cause burnout, and you could end up hating exercise, which will give you an excuse to skip your workouts.

I trick my brain by breaking my target down.

So instead of saying I am going to do 20 reps, I tell myself that I'm going to do five reps, just four times.

You can use the same tactic when it comes to sales targets.

If you want to make a million in a year, that works at less than £20,000 per week.

As the old saying goes – **'How do you eat an elephant? One bite at a time.'**

Tell yourself you are a morning exerciser: Keep telling yourself this until you are.

Your body listens to your thoughts.

Remember the wise words of Henry Ford?

If you believe you can't become a morning exerciser, you're setting yourself up for failure.

Tell yourself you love exercising in the morning and that it's easy and rewarding.

PREPARE FOR SUCCESS: Get your workout gear ready the night before - that way you won't be distracted from your goal. I have even heard of some people who sleep in their workout clothes so they can just jump out of bed and get it done without distractions!

Set your alarm an hour earlier than usual: Congratulations - you just bought yourself an extra hour in the day! Your exercise is not impinging on your previous schedule.

Also, locate your clock out of easy reach, so you have to get up out of bed to switch off the alarm.

If in doubt, set two alarm clocks! If you snooze you lose: Don't ignore your alarm in favour of a few more minutes under the duvet.

Aim to be out the door within 10 minutes of waking - that way; you will have less time to think of excuses not to exercise.

USE VISUALISATION: All top athletes use this skill to help motivate them because your mind cannot differentiate between what actually happened and what you visualised.

So before you go to bed, take time to think about the details of your perfect morning routine.

BEAT IT: Music is a proven motivator, so use it to your advantage. Create a playlist of whatever songs get you moving and get you psychologically pumped. Listen to audiobooks and podcasts so you can train your mind.

Plan your workout: Don't be vague as it makes it too easy to put off your training for another day.

Creating a consistent routine allows you to stick to your commitments.

Choose an exercise you enjoy doing so you don't start making excuses to quit.

Use what I have already taught you about being a disruptor and cut your own path and if the gym or running is not your thing – find what is. It could be pilates or a high energy sport.

Record your workouts so you can see how your performance is improving every day you work at it.

Don't just take my word for it.

Science proves that waking up earlier will change your life.

The research shows that if you exercise in the morning, you will be happier, more reliable and emotionally stable, have a lower risk of being stressed and overweight and you will be a better problem-solver.

Morning exercise helps increase fat burn, reduces unnecessary calorie consumption and lowers your blood pressure.

So what's your excuse not to do it?

You can regenerate every day by being exceptional from the moment you wake up!

YOU CAN THANK ME LATER!

The other daily practice that I recommend you start your day with for maximum thought regeneration is gratitude.

Sure it's easy to be grateful when you get a job promotion or even a beautiful gift.

Saying thank you is socially expected in such circumstances.

I bet you are thinking how could something so simple bring massive transformation in your life?

Well, you might be surprised to learn studies carried out by eminent psychologist and author Robert Emmons have proved that the benefits of practising genuine gratitude are extensive and wide-ranging.

In a series of studies which spanned over a decade, he helped over 1000 people systematically cultivate gratitude.

The results showed that people who mindfully practised gratitude for just three weeks overwhelmingly reported a host of benefits, including:

Physical
• Stronger immune systems
• Less physical pains

- Lower blood pressure
- Take better care of their health
- Feel more refreshed upon waking

Psychological
- Higher levels of positive emotions
- More alert, alive, and awake
- More joy and pleasure
- More optimism and happiness

Social
- More helpful, generous, and compassionate
- More forgiving
- More outgoing
- Feel less lonely and isolated.

THE AWESOME POWER OF THANK YOU

Here's my advice, my friend - cancel your personal pity parties today!

They cost you dearly in so many ways, and nobody is having a good time – least of all you.

If you're always stressed and ungrateful, you risk losing clients and employees, and valuable opportunities which will pass you by.

You are also harming your relationships with your family and friends, so stop focusing on the negative.

Who wants to be in the company of a constant whiner or complainer with nothing positive on their agenda?

Would you actively seek to spend time or work with that sort of person?   No – so don't be that person.

Be a winner, not a whiner.

Instead, imagine how you can harness all the benefits listed above free of charge in a really short space of time if you simply discipline yourself to practice gratitude every morning.

I write two pages of gratitude statements every morning and I make a point of saying thank you at every opportunity during the day.

I do this because I know and have experienced the incredible and life-changing power of being genuinely thankful.

Try it for just 21 days, and you will be amazed by how it regenerates your attitude to life.

There are two components to proactively regenerating your life through gratitude.

The first is that it is an affirmation that there are millions of good things in the world.

I am not naïve, and I know more than most people that the journey through life is not always a smooth and straight one.

It comes with a lot of stress and unwanted hassle. That happens to everyone but what will make you exceptional is how you handle adversity.

Practising gratitude every day reminds me these are just bumps in the road and they don't have to derail your progress altogether.

When you look at the whole picture of your life, gratitude encourages you to notice all the little quiet, positives in life that too often get drowned out by big, noisy negativity.

The second part of the power of gratitude is that it allows us to acknowledge that other people - or even higher powers - provide many gifts to help us achieve success in our lives.

Gratitude also gives you space to appreciate and live in the moment.

For example, if you take time to express your thanks for nature, you will stop and really appreciate a beautiful sunset.

On a summer's day, you will notice the sound of the birds and bees.

These small moments enrich your body and mind in ways you didn't even realise.

Gratitude gently forces you to stop and understand the value of something, therefore, extracting more benefits from it because you are less likely to take it for granted.

It helps you refocus on what resources you have instead of what you lack.

In fact, I believe gratitude is fundamental for personal and professional success because it allows you to be an active participant in your life, rather than just a spectator.

As you notice and focus more on the positives things in your life, you will begin to appreciate their real value and your attitude will be continually regenerated and revitalised.

In other words, gratitude magnifies the pleasures you get from life.

It's literally a secret shortcut to the positivity which drives the success you so crave.

Gratitude is a magic shield that blocks toxic, negative emotions, such as envy, resentment, regret and even depression.

Such negative emotions undermine your happiness and can destroy your motivation to be exceptional.

Get as much gratitude out into the Universe as you can. Say thank you in a sincere way for everything you have and to everyone that helps you.

Use every moment you can to be grateful. It can be as simple as saying thank you in your head for every rep you do in the gym or if you are driving, silently express your gratitude for green lights and parking spaces.

The phenomenal power of gratitude has been acknowledged since the dawn of time. Still, somehow in our fast-paced modern culture, we have forgotten to harness it.

According to ancient Chinese philosopher Lao Tzu, gratitude is vital because: **'When you realise nothing is lacking, the whole world belongs to you.'**

I want the whole world!

Don't you?

That's why I go through my gratitude list every morning without fail.

It helps me regenerate my positivity and alter my mindset to be ready for the day.

And these amazing results are not just based on my personal experience, as I have indicated above they are backed by solid science and high-level research.

Robert Emmons studies have scientifically proved you cannot feel envious and grateful at the same time because they're incompatible feelings.

It stands to reason that if you're grateful, you can't resent someone for having something that you don't.

Those are very different ways of relating to the world which underpins your attitude and actions.

His findings show that those who have high levels of gratitude have low levels of resentment and envy.

They are also more stress-resistant because they have perspective and a greater sense of self-worth.

Are you convinced yet why you should practice gratitude?   If not, let me explain the direct and impressive consequences of this simple action.

Gratitude will improve your productivity and the productivity of the people your business relies on.

It will open doors to new and rewarding personal and professional relationships.

It creates a frame of mind where you will naturally connect on a deeper level with clients, (both established and new business,) and you will develop beneficial relations with your suppliers and contractors.

Showing appreciation is also one of the most effective ways to motivate your employees. It's a straightforward equation that so many business leaders seem to forget when they disconnect from their staff.

So let me go over it again. When people feel valued, they feel good.

And when you make people feel good, they are more loyal and work harder for you.

Gratitude will help you get more sales because it heightens your mood and makes you instantly more personable.

Customers want to buy from salespeople they know, like and trust and when you are more relatable, your customers will like and trust you more.

If clients and customers feel appreciated, then they become loyal to your brand and keep coming back for repeat business.

Gratitude will change your brain.

Yes – you read that right.

Expressing gratitude in a meaningful and honest way will rewire the neural channels in your brain.

The hypothalamus is the part of our brain that regulates core bodily functions including appetite, sleep, temperature, metabolism and growth.

A study in 2009 showed it's stimulated and activated when we feel gratitude indicating that as human beings, we literally can't function without it.

Being grateful sounds easy, right?

Remember to say thanks from time to time – how hard can that be?

Forget that.

What I am talking about is seriously practising gratitude every day.

The keyword here is practising.

To regenerate your wellbeing and build a strong foundation for your empire of success, you need to actively participate in expressing gratitude every day in a planned, structured and accountable way.

TOM'S TOP TIPS FOR REGENERATIVE DAILY GRATITUDE

If you want to be exceptional, you need to work hard to turbo-charge the positive effects of being grateful. Let me explain how to be exceptionally grateful.

Firstly, you need to be honest about your feelings and reactions as there is a big difference in just saying thank you for the sake of good manners and actually feeling genuine gratitude.

Secondly, you must commit to gratitude practice every day. Like physical exercise, your powers of gratitude can be built up with regular and committed training.

Keep a gratitude journal. Write at least five things that you're thankful for every day. Don't worry if repetitive elements are occurring every day; the simple rule is if you're grateful for it, put it in your journal.

The more you write, the more you will enjoy writing.

In your journal you have the complete freedom to express yourself without judgement because you are the only one reading it.

This is a great way to have a conversation with yourself and explore your inner thoughts and motivations.

Throughout the day, think about what you have listed in your journal. Remind yourself often how these things have benefited your life.

Practice gratitude. Put it into action by finding ways to thank people for something they did that you appreciate.

You will enjoy the glow of kindness because you have made them feel better! They will feel a greater connection to you, and then you have set up a positivity loop.

Swap frustrations for thanks.

What should you be grateful for?   **EVERYTHING!!**

Only you know what you appreciate most in your life, but here are ten things to stimulate your own gratitude:

1. **Your life** – You have survived this far when so many didn't.

2. **Your family** – Appreciate the lifelong relationships you enjoy.

3. **Your friends** – They are the people who always have your back.

4. **Your joy** – Think of all the things that make you smile.

5. **Your failures** - Be grateful for the wisdom that your mistakes have taught you.

6. **Your mentors** – Say thanks to all the people who took time to support and guide you.

7. **Your body and mind** – They are yours alone to command.

8. **Your simple pleasures** – A cup of tea, a great meal, having a laugh, or even a comfy chair.

9. **Your career** – Your job, even if you want to upgrade, has provided you with security.

10. **Your memories** – Be grateful for all your past experiences as they have made you who you are.

Remember, as you read this book and master my unique Five Golden Principles of Dream to Achieve, the more successful you will become and the more you will have to be grateful for!

Mission Statement

You cannot solve your problems with the same level of thinking that created them.

You are the only person who can make this happen.

TOM'S TIPS FOR REGENERATION

- You must raise your level of thinking to exceptional if you want to perform that way.
- Get out of your comfort zone.
- All past mistakes and successes are over, and their energy is spent.
- Change is the thing that keeps us interested and engaged with life.
- You are the scriptwriter in the blockbuster of your life, so make yourself the hero.
- Ignore everyone else's perception of how things are done and make your own rules.
- Nothing is impossible.
- An upset in the status quo can deliver dividends, but only if you are prepared to grab them.
- Be confident enough to be a disruptor.
- A positive mindset will give you more confidence, improve your mood and open your mind to the possibilities.
- Be exceptional from the moment you wake up! Set up a positive early morning routine underpinned by practising gratitude and physical exercise to stimulate your metabolism.

DREAM

Chapter 3: Energisation

I give thanks every day that I am a powerhouse of pure energy.

Through my conscious dedication to the practice of being exceptional, I continually monitor and keep my mind and body finely tuned and in energy alignment.

It gives me all the focus and stamina I need to achieve my full potential, regardless of what I am working on.

And guess what?

The good news is you also have such an engine, but it has probably been neglected for decades because you have just taken it for granted.

You just didn't notice it because it's been ticking over and idling away in the background - underperforming.

I have found there's a direct connection between the right energy and the right results.

I'm teaching you how to become an expert mechanic so you can tune your internal engine up to top performance every day.

I'm giving you the spark plugs, turbo-boosters and nitro kit to make sure you are always on the winners' podium.

I'm revealing my secrets of being exceptional to help you turn your old tractor engine into a brand-new Lamborghini!

If you don't believe it's possible, just remember that Ferruccio Lamborghini started his company in 1948 with tractor manufacturing and didn't build his first sports car until the mid-1960s!

The secret key you need to start your high-performance mental engine is a positive attitude underpinned by endless energy.

Let me share an important observation with you based on my own experience of running numerous successful businesses.

No matter what project you embark on, it will take more energy to complete successfully than you ever anticipate. Sometimes 10 or even 100 times more!

That's because, at the planning stage of any venture, we focus only on the positive aspects and fail to prepare our reserves of energy to overcome the challenges.

Inevitably you are going to face ups and downs in the economy, resistance to change, poor finance flow and staff problems.

Energy and resilience are essential if you want to weather the storm while powering your ship through it.

You are the captain, and it's your job to steer the vessel.

As leader, you are setting the tone for everyone else.

So if you don't put in maximum effort, don't be surprised when your staff copy your unenergetic example.

The truth is your vibe influences your tribe.

So don't just coast through life. Refuse to accept other people who are happy to drift along without effort.

Imagine if you were heading up a rowing crew in a racing boat and just one member of the team wasn't pulling their weight.

Your boat would drift off course and fall behind all competitors in the race.

Other crew members would lose focus and determination.

Your forward momentum would be fatally disrupted.

The same principle applies in business.

There's no room for lack of effort, and all bluffers should be cast overboard before they sink you.

Always remember the difference between success and failure is attitude, and that comes from the energy you self-generate.

But believe me, the effort is always worth it in the end.

Nothing beats the feeling of completing a project successfully knowing you have put in maximum effort. It's the world's best legal high!

Let me share an example of how my DREAM system of success influences and drives my energy and motivation every day of my life, regardless of what I am doing.

I was on holiday recently on the Greek island of Santorini, which is famous for its steep set of 587 steps from the old port to Fira.

Such is the incline, the trip to the top is generally only made by donkeys.

I chose to run the steps – not once but four times!   Even though I was on holiday and the locals told me it was impossible.

Why?

To remind myself there is no such thing as a day off for exceptional people.

To prove to myself that I could.

To push my self-belief.

To give 100 per cent and more to my chosen task.

And to underline to myself that I am exceptional.

Those stone steps up the mountain were a metaphor of the uphill climb of life that you need to excel at every day.

Every step was a challenge. Every step was an obstacle.

As I ran up, my heart thudding in my chest, over and over, I repeated my mantra for success – D-determination, R-Regeneration, E-Energization, A-Ambition, M- motivation.

I had to conquer those steps before the sun rose and set on Santorini.

And I did.

I proved I could overcome anything I put my mind to, and it felt amazing!

With application, you can do the same.

I use extreme fitness sessions to improve not just my body but also my mind because it helps me reinforce my 'never give up' attitude.

Using exercise helps me not only shape and sculpt my body but also my attitude and this is massively beneficial to my whole life.

BE AN EXTREMIST

My belief that extreme thoughts, extreme behaviour, extreme discipline and extreme effort are required to be an exceptional person is validated by some of the most successful people in the world.

But you need extreme entrepreneurial energy to maintain extreme levels of discipline.

That's why you need to be obsessed.

Obsession is what lazy people call dedication.

To be a success, your focus needs to be so obsessive that other people think you are genuinely crazy.

Apple founder and entrepreneurial genius Steve Jobs said: **'You can quote them, disagree with them, glorify or vilify them, but the only thing you can't do is ignore them because they change things. They push the human race forward, and while some may see them as the crazy ones, we see genius, because the people who are crazy enough to think that they can change the world, are the ones who do.'**

Being average requires dedication - but being exceptional requires obsession.

Obsession is defined as 'the domination of one's thoughts or feelings by a persistent idea, image, or desire.'

Ultimate Fighting Championship's supreme Irish warrior Conor McGregor once said: **'This is an obsession. Talent does not exist; we are all equals as human beings. You could be anyone if you put in the time... I am not talented; I am obsessed.'**

All champions and billionaires know that if you want success, you need to be obsessed.

Just being a workaholic is not enough – you need to invest your soul into the project you believe in.

Here's what being obsessed with success will do for you:

65

• It will make you brave – when you are obsessed, you are not scared to start a project and drive it through to completion.

• It will help you have more groundbreaking thoughts – if you are obsessed with something, you think about it all the time, and that's when you have new insights that will give you an edge over your competition.

• It will direct your focus – being obsessed will energise your every action. When you are always thinking about new opportunities and innovation, you will discover better ways of doing business.

• It will help you take personal responsibility – if you want to learn from both success and failure, obsession means you own the outcome.

• It will help you become a problem solver: Obsession makes you continue to look for solutions when everyone else has given up.

• It will make you committed to achieving your dreams – you are more likely to stick with your plans after the non-obsessed give up.

GO BIG OR GO HOME

I have learned that you need to treat every action, every thought and every deal as though your life depends on it, because it does.

Take massive actions to achieve massive results.

What does massive action mean?

It means doing far more than the average person would do under similar conditions and going further than anyone would typically expect of you or anyone else.

It means thinking big and acting to achieve those goals with focused energy.

It means challenging and upgrading your personal standards.

It means consistently following through on your thoughts and actions.

To become an expert at anything, it takes at least 10,000 hours of investment in study and practice.

Would you expect to be perfectly fit after one session at the gym?

No – of course, you wouldn't!

And it's the same if you want to be an exceptional, high-achieving individual. You need to practice and stick at it.

You need to plan ahead, use your skills to visualise your success and then put all your effort into achieving your goals.

You must generate the right energy to be fearless.

You can't become a champion overnight.

It takes years of work and discipline, and 100 per cent effort, 100 per cent of the time.

Ask yourself this – are you just a contender or a winner?

Are you ready to accept the challenge to become exceptional?

Are you genuinely committed to my DREAM system?

Are you working hard enough to become fearless?

HARNESS THE RIGHT ENERGY

I can honestly tell you that every business deal I have done has involved a lot more calls, meetings, emails, legal work and general running around than I ever anticipated.

But what kept me going was being able to generate the right energy, regardless of the challenges.

Let me give you an example.

When I started my Dream Luxury Serviced Apartments concept back in 2017 after returning from Dubai full of inspiration, I began from a standing start.

My keys strengths were determination, energy and ambition.

I chased every single opportunity looking for just the right building to launch my business idea.

I went to practically every city in the UK and had doors closed in my face, hundreds of messages and emails never responded to and many, many calls ignored.

I must have got a thousand 'Nos' before I got a single 'Yes'.

I was new to the business, and nobody knew me, so I was easy to ignore.

Or so they thought!

It felt like there was a 12-inch-thick sheet of ice blocking me from even starting on my epic journey of success.

But I was driven by an energy that would not let me stop or fail.

I began hitting that wall of ice with a pick-axe of determination.

At first, nothing happened.

But I just kept hitting it with increasing levels of energy.

Then tiny cracks appeared.

I didn't allow myself to become disheartened, and I relied on sheer grit to power me through.

In fact, with every setback, I upped my energy levels until the ice sheet shattered and allowed opportunity to flow my way.

Getting knocked down 1000 times does not matter as long as you have developed the right energy to get up 1001 times.

Then, like now, I have an apex predator mentality.

I prowled like a shark waiting on the right opportunity to arise.

And when it did, I pounced immediately and got the building that I wanted to launch my first dream project.

Three years later, I now have a property portfolio numbering in the hundreds across the world.

So what fueled my success from starting with nothing to being one of the top serviced accommodation providers in the UK?

The right energy to keep going and keep me pushing harder and harder until I got what I wanted.

I learned that success does not come overnight.

Stay hungry or be hungry – it's your choice.

You have to keep hitting the obstacle with increasing energy levels until you can breakthrough.

When you are starting, you must quickly figure out how to get past the gatekeepers to reach the real decision-makers.

Powerful and successful people employ a small army of staff like PAs, secretaries and managers to keep you out of their world.

They don't need you, but you need them.

So you need to be totally determined to reach them, and if that means parachuting onto the roof and abseiling down the side of the building to get a meeting with them, you must be prepared to do that!

Keep punching until you break through, keep contacting people until you get an appointment, keeping looking for the right connection to make it work for you.

Don't make 100 calls, make 1000 and increase your odds of success.

Keep going until you turn 'no' into 'yes'.

Then one day the same people who blanked you at the start of your journey will be trying to get an appointment with you.

Imagine the sense of satisfaction you will enjoy when that happens!

WHAT IS ENERGY?

Energy is defined as the capacity to perform work.

According to the First Law of Thermodynamics, the total amount of energy in the Universe is constant — incapable of being created or destroyed.

It can only change from one form to another.

You have the internal capacity to change your energy from negative to positive to fuel your transformation and power your work.

As we discussed in the previous chapter, physical energy comes through mental and physical fitness.

Now you are working on those through my DREAM system; I bet you can already see and feel the changes?

Energy is core and baseline when it comes to being exceptional.

You are now changing your personal energy through your actions.

Think of all the ways you can practically support your external and internal transformation.

For example, consider the energy you are putting into your 'success engine' in the form of food.

A delicious, moderate, healthy diet will be processed efficiently and advantageously by your body, so eat mindfully for good energy.

Junk food makes junk thoughts.

You wouldn't put dirty fuel in a performance sports car, would you?

Nor would you run it on an empty tank, so make sure you get a good night's sleep every night.

The body and mind need rest to recharge.

So as you are planning an early start to get in your exercise and gratitude practice before you begin work, go to bed earlier to ensure you get a night of sufficient, regenerative sleep.

Small adjustments in your daily routine are already helping to tune your energy engine for success.

Now we are going to work on the internal energy you need to generate to be exceptional.

BE LIKE THE SUN

Everything is made of energy including every atom, molecule, cell and system in the human body.

So it is essential to always keep a check on the energy you are generating.

Every morning an alert beeps at 4.05am – its set to go off five minutes after I wake up.

The message displayed is simple – 'Are you in alignment, Tom?'

This alarm is set to jolt me into the right energy mode for the day.

It reminds me to check that all the mental and physical tools I need for my daily success are working harmoniously.

I've learned that if you are not in proper alignment, you won't emit or attract the right energy.

Why do you need to check it every day and keep yourself on point?

Because nobody else will.

You must do this when you first wake up so you can set the dial on your day to positive.

To promote alignment, meditate and visualise your goals for the day ahead.

Breathe in the positive and breathe out the negative.

Be grateful and affirm your thanks for all that you are.

When you awake in the morning, take a moment to think of what a precious privilege, it is just to be alive and healthy.

Say thank you as you wake up and as soon as your feet hit the floor.

Remind yourself you have the power to dictate how your day is going to pan out.

Be confident that you can flick the energy switch from negative to positive anytime you want.

Developing this skill will improve your mental recovery time when you have had a negative experience.

But it takes time to master and I will explore this in more depth in my second book entitled 'Whatever It Takes' which is set to be released in Summer 2021.

I had my first harsh lesson in energy switching when my daughter was very young and my relationship with her mum ended.

I was upset by not having daily contact with my beloved child whom I was 100 per cent dedicated to.

I lost all focus because the anxiety and negativity were draining my energy.

It began to affect all parts of my life, including my health, my work and even my relationship with the child I adored because she was picking up on my negative energy.

I vividly remember pushing my little girl on a swing in the park one day while hiding my tears behind a pair of dark glasses so as not to upset her.

I was spiralling and seeking something to save me.

I subconsciously reached out to the Universe, and it delivered exactly what I needed.

My wife, Dolores, lent me 'The Secret' by Rhonda Byrne, which introduced me to the Law of Attraction and I am forever grateful that I read this book.

This is the principle that you attract whatever you focus your energy on (good or bad).

This book taught me how to speak the language of the Universe, which is energy vibration.

I realised I had to actively change my energy to change my outcomes.

So every day I didn't see my baby girl, I would set aside time to look at beautiful and happy photographs of her on my phone.

I visualised us having a fantastic time the next time we were together.

I projected into the future the fantastic relationship we would have as she grew up.

I rejected all negative connotations.

I consciously changed my energy so I could work positively towards the result I wanted.

And it worked.

I had wonderful times with my daughter when she was young and have gone on to develop a fantastic relationship with her as a young adult.

But through the initial pain of separation, I learned that the energy of your thoughts creates your reality.

So you must become conscious of all your thoughts.

I took the time to realign my thoughts and emotions.

Only then could I change my energy and take control of everything else.

This experience was more than 12 years ago, and it changed my life.

It made me realise the power of my mindset and the importance of bringing the right energy to every situation.

Everything you say, think or feel becomes your reality so vibrate your energy to the highest levels of positivity.

It's all about vibrational alignment with the Universe and harmony of mind, body and spirit to that frequency.

Alignment of body and mind has been promoted and practiced in Eastern medicine for thousands of years.

Once you are aware of the importance of mindset to every aspect of your life, you will become more conscious about controlling it.

TAKE CONTROL

'You have power over your mind – not outside events. Realise this, and you will find strength.'

This profound quote by Roman Emperor Marcus Aurelius tells you that everything is a matter of perspective.

Control your thoughts, and you control your world.

Change your words, and you change your world.

You have the power to change your perspective through positive energisation.

You are doing it already by following my Dream to Achieve program.

Remember - what you generate, you radiate.

Project your positivity through your speech and body language.

When you walk into a room, learn to dominate it with your shining persona and high vibrational energy.

Your positivity should shine from you like the sun on a summer's day and have the same effect on you and the those you encounter.

Sprinkle stardust everywhere you go and use your presence to project positive energy.

Here is an example of what I mean.

We all accept that airports can be a stressful place to navigate and the energy within them is often tense.

I frequently travel through London, Liverpool and Manchester airports, and one day I asked an official-looking man at the security check if he was in charge.

Immediately, he was defensive as he expected me to start complaining.

Instead, I pointed out that I am a frequent flyer through the airport, and it was always a pleasure to interact with his team as they are courteous, efficient and effective.

He was genuinely shocked, but he smiled at my unusual positivity, and as I put my shoes on, I watched him walk over to his staff and convey my message.

I observed the smile I had gifted the supervisor spread around the whole team, and it felt amazing that I had made so many people feel appreciated – even for a moment.

They all looked over and waved to say thanks. I left with a spring in my step, and the energy dial of the whole security team was moved into the positive zone.

It cost nothing and paid dividends so just do it when you can.

'Pretend that every single person you meet has a sign around his or her neck that says, 'Make me feel important.' Not only will you succeed in sales, but you will also succeed in life.' - Mary Kay Ash

The opposite of this positive mindset is repelling.

Don't be a dark cloud of negativity ready to rain on somebody's parade.

You must have experienced picking up on 'bad energy' from somebody else, right?

Did it make you want to work with them or spend time with them?

NO – in fact, you probably ran in the opposite direction!

That's because a person's energy will tell you more about them than what they say or do.

I learned this valuable lesson when I was in my mid-20s and working as head of security for a popular nightclub in downtown Belfast which attracted all strata of society.

Before the ceasefire in Northern Ireland, Belfast clubs and pubs' door security staff routinely faced potentially lethal threats every time they went to work.

Disgruntled punters had the potential to take your life or put a price on your head if you mishandled the situation.

My security team and I were sitting targets for would-be assassins with serious form.

We had to rely on our wits and the right energy to stay alive.

This illuminating experience provided me with a dangerous education into all aspects of the human character.

It certainly helped me build the level of fearlessness that has directly lead to my current success.

Being able to read an individual's energy became an essential tool for literally saving my life.

Here is an example of what I mean.

I was in charge of security at one of the hottest nightclubs in Belfast. Every week it featured superstar DJs blasting House Music to throngs of Belfast's beautiful people.

It was packed with gorgeous girls and fashionable guys drinking champagne and cocktails and access to the VIP area was in high demand.

I was working as head of security in this fantastic club when I found myself on the wrong side of an escalating fight with a guy who had just been released from prison after serving a life sentence for multiple murders.

This man had serious connections to organised crime and a notorious reputation for extreme violence.

Along with about 10 of his friends, he had unfortunately turned up at this club to celebrate being freed from jail.

I was forced to deny his group access, and that's when their aggressive behaviour at the door of the club began to intensify.

My security team were desperately holding the door closed to bar their entry and were genuinely thought they could be shot.

Our particular security team had a hard-won reputation for being the toughest in the city.

This could all go wrong very quickly, and the result could be fatal.

To save lives and cool the situation down, I knew I had to go it alone and change the dynamic and energy.

So I told my team to open the door and let me out into the baying mob, then lock the door behind me, and no matter what happened, they were not to open it.

They thought I was mad and begged me not to go on a suicide mission. But I went.

I pulled up my shoulders, walked straight out, identified the dominant leader of the party and shook his hand.

I engaged without aggression and showed a willingness to listen and understand.

This action won me instant respect because I had the sheer audacity to step out and face them alone.

I had the brains and fearlessness to take control and direct the situation in my favour.

I didn't give them access to the club and they left without incident.

This was only achievable because I instinctively knew how to read and project human energy.

I always used my skills for reading peoples' energy to get critical non-verbal cues.

By feeling the vibe punters were giving off, I was able to anticipate trouble and make early interventions to stop it escalating.

It made me very effective at my job because I was able to neutralise bad energy before it exploded into violence.

I was also able to utilise my own positive energy to alter and counter the negativity of people who stepped up to challenge me.

It wasn't about being aggressive. Any fool can do that!

It was about being able to project an aura of authority and invincibility.

To simply be a powerhouse without having to play-act at being one.

This is how you become a leader.

Don't kid yourself you are a good leader simply because you are the head of the company or because you got a promotion to management.

You are only a good leader when you dare to go first and lead by example.

Exceptional leaders are the:

- First to go towards the danger.
- First to take the risks.
- First to trust without expecting trust back.
- First to give difficult feedback to help people grow and improve.
- First to take responsibility for the team and their results.

That's why I bring the energy of fearlessness I learned while working in a club in Belfast 25 years ago into the boardroom.

I know if I can face down and win over convicted killers, I can't be intimidated when it comes to making a deal.

People who think they are tough negotiators pale in comparison to what I have already faced during my life and career.

I can create an energy that tells people I am invincible and unstoppable.

You must learn to do the same by drawing on your own experiences and learning to underpin your supreme confidence.

When you can learn to translate and understand it, you will realise the importance of the energy field that everybody is subconsciously transmitting.

This should act as a reminder that you are continually projecting an energy field yourself that others can feel.

And you certainly don't want to generate, then radiate the sort of energy that blocks opportunities for success.

The good thing is since most people tend to be negative, your exceptional positivity will make you stand out from the crowd in every circumstance.

It will make you a beacon for success because the right people will actively want to work with you.

You should develop a reputation for your positive attitude, unlimited energy and as a person who gets things done.

Old-school core values of actually doing what you say you are going to do are worth their weight in gold.

People with good intentions make promises but people with good character keep them.

Reliability is priceless because it's a surprisingly rare commodity.

Clients and collaborators will have more confidence in your ability to deliver a project successfully when they know you give 100 per cent of your high levels of energy to everything you do.

Be a person who under-promises but over-delivers. Definitely not the other way round.

Be proud to have honour and make your word mean something every time.

Positive energy is infectious, and your upbeat attitude will transform whomever you are interacting with.

It's more memorable and influential than you can ever imagine.

For example, I was on holiday in Mexico, and every morning I would ask Fredrico the waiter how he was feeling that morning.

And every day he replied with a huge smile "Excelente, Mr Smyth, Excelente!"

That simple interaction has stuck with me for years because Fredrico wasn't just 'struggling by' or 'doing ok' or even 'doing good'.

No, every day he was telling himself, me and the Universe that he was 'Excelente'.

His positive energy was infectious and memorable.

That's how powerful the right energy can be no matter what the circumstances.

In my experience, it smooths the way ahead in any relationship but is particularly useful when it comes to sales – and remember you are always selling yourself when it comes to opportunity.

You have the power to control how others respond by controlling how you present yourself.

With the force of your personal energy, you can and will and turn a negative into a positive, a no into a yes with startling regularity.

Your customers and clients will want to speak to you.

If you start a call with a smile on your face and good energy in your voice, your potential customer is more likely to smile and feel positive about your interaction.

That's an easier starting position for conversion that could lead to a sale or the deal of a lifetime.

Energy flows from the top. Your energy sets the agenda for every interaction.

Too many times, leaders, entrepreneurs and managers believe attitude and energy are outside of their control.

In fact, it is the complete opposite.

They're not. You can start every workday, every call and every project, go all-in with your energy, your enthusiasm, and your excitement regardless of how frustrated or depressed you feel about the circumstances around you.

'Let's face it; if you can't control your energy, it will prove very difficult to control much of anything in life or in business.' - Grant Cardone

In my industry, the personal energy of my entire team is my most valuable business asset.

That's why I work on my own and my staff's energy every day.

No matter what needs to be said in our team meetings, I always make sure my staff go out with a positive mindset and their self-belief bolstered.

Let me explain.

When it comes to serviced apartments, my staff often form more personal relationships with guests than they would at a hotel because they are the main point of contact for everything guests need, especially if they are enjoying an extended stay for weeks or even months.

My staff become the guests' staff while they are staying in my properties.

These interactions are the energy engine of my entire business empire.

I can't be there personally to oversee every interaction, so I need to be confident that my team represent my values and my ethos at all times.

This is crucial to the success of my business. This is why you must take your energisation seriously.

Hospitality expert and TV star Anthony Melchiorri notes: **'You can have all the marble in the world and butler service, but if you have rude people that don't take care of guests' needs, you don't have anything.'**

HOW TO BE A NUCLEAR GENERATOR OF POSITIVE ENERGY

So now let's look at how you can improve your vital life force to power you the level of being exceptional.

Body Talk

Let's start with the basics.

First impressions last, so how you look is essential when it comes to projecting positive energy.

I don't mean that you need to have movie star or supermodel looks to be a success (but it sometimes helps in life!).

Natural beauty is like winning the jackpot in the genetic lottery, and you can't control that.

But what you can control is how you present yourself.

Remember the old adage - Natural beauty is only skin deep.

You could be a beautiful person on the outside, but an ugly attitude will always shine through.

Your face is your fortune as it's the first thing people will notice about you, and it's how they will remember you.

Your smile could be literally worth a million dollars.

So smile more, even when you have to fake it.

And say 'Yes' a lot more – you can't help but smile when you are responding positively.

Body language often communicates much more than words, so actively keep your physical conversation positive.

Walk tall and present yourself with confidence and openness.

Don't slouch or lounge around with slumped shoulders and your hands stuffed in your pockets.

Or worse still, with your arms folded defensively across your chest.

Your body language can be screaming 'get away from me!' to all potential opportunities without you even realising it.

Look like you are always ready for action.

You are your own brand and how you present yourself is your advertising billboard.

Dress for success.

Treat every interaction like a job interview.

There's a good reason why you prepare in advance when you know you are going to be assessed for a job.

You want to present the best version of yourself in every way - from how you look, to what you say.

Dressing sharp will change the way you view yourself and the way others view you.

Dress in a manner that suggests that you are proud, prepared and confident of success.

In other words, if you are going to the bank, dress like you own it.

People appreciate it when you make an effort to look professional.

If you want to be exceptional, perform every day with the same level of care and energy you would present to a potential employer who you are trying to impress.

PRESSING ENGAGEMENTS

Always have an engaging project you are working - busy people don't have time to waste on negativity.

Keep your activity levels high and seek new, positive challenges.

You always need to be learning more about yourself and the world and then converting that knowledge into actions that help you achieve the exceptional.

Read and stay curious so that you always have something positive and exciting to add to any conversation.

It's no coincidence that most of the world's top wealth owners are avid readers.

Good company always attracts good business as other people will enjoy spending time with you and will want to work collaboratively because they feed off your powerhouse of energy.

Act competently, be knowledgeable, exude success and be positive and optimistic, regardless of what is happening around you.

Potential customers are much more attracted to positive people.

Flip your thinking for a second.

Have you ever gone to a shop to buy something and left without purchasing anything because you experienced the crappy attitude or bad energy from an assistant?

I am sure you have. It's not because the staff were deliberately rude or confrontational.

It's because a person's attitude displays itself in much subtler ways, and as human beings, we are very attuned to read it.

You need to be aware of the energy you are projecting in all circumstances because, whether you realise it or not, this is having a profound impact on your ability to succeed.

Plan or Fail.

The adage is true – fail to plan, and you plan to fail.

You need a road map to keep you focused and energised about your journey to being exceptional.

You are always working toward 'staging points' rather than an end destination because as I have explained previously, success needs constant maintenance.

Don't focus on the negative energy of the problems you encounter.

Convert your energy to finding solutions for yourself and also for other people which you can sell to them!

Be the first into the office and the last out of it because you should be actively seeking new challenges all the time.

Your plan must be based on relentless determination and driven by a commitment not to give up or compromise your end goals.

THINK LIKE A BILLIONAIRE!

It is worth noting that even the super-wealthy only have 24 hours in the day - same as you!

What makes the self-made success story different and exceptional, (and thus allows them to access great wealth) is that they bring additional massive energy to every action in their life.

That's the same energy that you need to cultivate if you hope to emulate their success.

A 2019 American study, conducted for the Affluent Market Institute, which looked at the lives of 600 super-wealthy and successful people concluded the following:

• Millionaires and billionaires typically read, exercise, and work more, but spend less time on social media and fewer hours sleeping.

• Successful individuals are keenly aware of how they spend their resources, including their emotional and cognitive resources.

• Millionaires spend roughly five and a half hours a week reading for pleasure, compared to the average American's two hours.

• Millionaires also spend more time exercising — nearly six hours a week compared to the average American's weekly two and a half hours.

• Millionaires may have more time to exercise because they spend less time on social media. The average American spends 14 hours a week on social media compared to the average millionaires who spends just two hours per week checking it.

• Commitment to hard work and hustle exemplifies another trait common amongst millionaires. They often work more than the average American — a difference of six hours per week.

The overall findings of this study revealed that the two most common traits you need to become rich are resilience and perseverance, and it takes conscious effort to develop these skills.

That's what my unique Five Golden Principles of Dream to Achieve are teaching you right now. The bottom line is, to be exceptional, you need to be goal-orientated and willing to put in more work than everyone else, and that needs good energy to make it sustainable.

From a personal perspective, I start work at 4am and keep going as long as I need to.

Regularly, this means me working 16 to 18-hour days.

Luckily, I have a supportive wife and family who understand and celebrate my drive to be exceptional.

First thing every morning, I spend two hours working on myself with both physical and mental exercises while I wait on the rest of the world waking up and catching up with me.

Already, I have given myself an energy advantage to carry me through the long day.

The other six key elements, or 'wealth factors', for achieving success and wealth according to the study into the most successful self-made people in America are:

1. **Financial planning** – Rich people stay rich by living like they are poor. Poor people stay poor by living like they are rich! They don't waste money on crap just to be part of the current trend.

2. **360-degree confidence** – Self-made people have confidence when it comes to finance, leadership and personal control.

3. **Responsibility -** which involves accepting your role in financial outcomes and believing that simple luck does not exist.

4. **Planning -** or setting goals for your financial future.

5. **Focus -** on seeing tasks through to their completion without being distracted.

6. **Social indifference -** not succumbing to social pressure to buy the latest thing.

ESCAPE THE NEGATIVE VIBES

Through many challenging experiences, I have learned that life is too short to waste time wondering what other people think about you.

It will limit your thoughts and actions and drain all of the positive energy you are investing time generating.

People who are always unhappy and unsuccessful have one thing in common – they worry too much about what other people think.

I, on the other hand, don't.

By giving energy to such thoughts, you are essentially giving your power away to others.

The simple way to reclaim your power is to stop thinking too much about other people and instead, refocus your energy to things that matter.

Having spent a large part of my life in the construction and building sector, I love this next phrase which describes the type of energy others can bring to your life: **Life is made of two kinds of people – drains and radiators!**

My clear advice is to avoid the 'drains' and stay close to the 'radiators'.

Do an environment audit now!

Decontaminate all sources of negativity from your life.

Create an official 'no negativity zone' around you both professionally and personally.

Put up signs in your office to remind people that negativity is not tolerated.

You must create an environment that fuels your positive energy.

Surround yourself with people, images, speech and activities that make you feel good and keep you motivated so that your mental input is always positive.

Honestly, shut the door to negative people and negative attitudes as they will destroy your plans and your business.

Remember, you are picking up the tab for other people's negativity.

Is that a price you want to pay?

Think of negativity as a contagious virus, like Covid-19 - because that's what it is.

You would avoid those whom you know to be carriers.

You would shield yourself from infection.

You would build up your immunity so that you are resilient.

Bad news and negative energy are toxic – in fact, fatal to many of your plans and projects so protect and inoculate yourself from other peoples' negativity.

Just because other people don't have or have given up on their dreams doesn't mean you should share in their failure.

Negativity is a toxic swamp, and its victims will reach out and pull you into the quicksand with them.

Those people don't want you to succeed because your success proves them wrong.

When you achieve the impossible, lots of people are left standing around with egg on their faces!

And note – this will make them even more negative about you because you have exposed their weaknesses.

Take it as a compliment – the more they hate, the better you are doing.

Those same haters will, in time, become your followers.

I have heard people claim they are not negative but a 'realist'.

But they are referring to their reality, not yours.

Just ignore them and distance yourself from the weight of negativity that they are carrying around with them.

They don't want just to share their self-made burdens, but double them and give you their negativity.

Your upbeat, can-do, positive attitude directly challenges their version of reality and they cannot comprehend it.

Weak and overwhelmed individuals resort to criticism and the best revenge against your critics is huge success.

IF IT BLEEDS, IT LEADS!

The contagion of negativity is everywhere! Its draining energy seeps through the cracks of your everyday life pretty much unnoticed in the constant background noise of social media and news channels.

Its draining your positivity without you even realising it.

Remember, information is not neutral.

It's helpful to visualise information like the food you consume for fuel.

Always passively eating junk food will diminish the power of your body.

In the same way, consumption of junk information will destroy your energy and your attitude.

Unfortunately, we are all biologically programmed to seek out bad news in the same way we crave junk food.

This human weakness is good for those in the business of selling it.

The fact is sad but straightforward - bad news sells.

Negativity is big business.

That's why newspapers and broadcast media outlets tend to go big on disaster and failure.

They want your attention so they can sell their products.

You could be forgiven for forgetting that information and news are sellable commodities.

They have been wrapped around advertising platforms, so consumers are drawn in to look at products they didn't even know they needed!

We are conditioned at a primal level to take notice of the information that could threaten our personal safety.

Researchers refer to our collective desire to hear and remember bad news as 'negativity bias'.

We have evolved to react quickly to potential threats, so we notice bad news to avoid danger.

Think about it, would you pick up a newspaper if the headline screamed 'Everything Is All Right!'?

Without you even noticing, you are constantly bombarded by stories about war, crime, pollution and death, whether you want to be or not.

It's everywhere - on the TV, on your phone, on the computer and in publications. It's probably the first thing you see when you wake up and the last before you go to sleep.

This is continuously depleting your energy because you have to process disturbing facts without any way of influencing the outcome.

Manufacturers of news and global social media platforms are turning you into a zombie consumer so they can make money from pumping you with information that is literally bad for your health.

They need to scare and worry you into consumption.

If you live in the negative energy of fear, you will never achieve success.

Take my advice - detox this negativity out of your life.

Divert your full resources into generating the positive energy you need to be exceptional.

ANTI-SOCIAL MEDIA

Unfortunately, as long as bad things happen, (which will be forever), there will be negative information on your newsfeed.

This has been artificially amplified in the last decade because so many people have camera phones and internet access now and can now document and spread more bad news.

Trust me; you need to understand your newsfeed is mostly unreliable and irrelevant data.

It's a fog of information without analysis, organisation or editorial scrutiny.

I'm now starting my fourth year not watching the news. I rely on my staff to keep me up updated on a need to know basis about things that directly impact on my business interests.

I recently logged on to social media to check a news story that could have a direct effect on my business operations.

I was instantly hit by a huge wave of negativity in both the stories and the meaningless, uneducated and empty commentary of users.

I actually laughed out loud as I realised why I don't waste my time locked into the unproductive insanity of social media!

It is literally a joke! So don't let yourself become a sheep-media punchline.

Social media is a weapon of mass distraction!

It blocks your thought-process bandwidth and limits your abilities to think and act in your own best interests.

I have recognised and accepted that I am not getting a clear or accurate picture of what is relevant to my life, and that's why I haven't read or listened to the news for years.

I use social media as a tool to promote my business interests, rather than letting it use me as a tool to make money for somebody else selling worthless information.

I find people are often shocked and surprised when I say I don't watch the news or that I'm not logged into social media constantly.

Do I feel like I am missing out on anything?

Nope – not at all.

Do I need people I don't know to 'like' my posts to build up my ego?   No.

Do I genuinely care about other people's holidays or what their Christmas decorations look like?   No.

Think about it – do you?

I have concluded it's just a relentless torrent of irrelevant negativity that pollutes and dilutes my positive energy.

It seems universally accepted that everyone should be plugged into the news agenda at all times.

That just shows you how good the media is at controlling and influencing how people think and behave.

It's a clear example of why you should aspire to be exceptional rather than the same as everyone else.

A different perspective often affords better insight.

'I think there should be regulations on social media to the degree that it negatively affects the public good.' - Elon Musk

TIMES HAVE CHANGED

For decades in Northern Ireland during the Troubles, our entire community was obsessed with hearing and reading the news.

It was a natural reaction because the conflict was right on our doorsteps.

Events like shooting and bombings directly impacted on our family and friends.

Our lives depended on accurate information on where it was safe to travel.

News and information were genuinely tools for survival in a civil war situation where danger was close and real.

Now the material conditions have changed, I don't have to do that anymore.

I don't need to be plugged into stress and negativity all day.

The news is not saving my life these days; it's actually undermining it.

Can you honestly say the information you are spending lots of your precious time consuming is life-changing, protecting or enhancing?

Stop and really think about the majority of the content on your relentless streams of social media.

Micro-stories affecting very few people get blown out of proportion when they 'go viral'.

Irrelevant 'celebrities' take up way too much airtime flaunting their lifestyles/problems, pets, kids or whatever they are trying to sell you.

People with no expertise or experience get public platforms for their baseless opinions.

But here is an important insight to remember - all this does not happen by accident.

Your viewing and valuable time are being manipulated for someone's else gain.

Without realising it, you have become the product.

You are working at wasting time.

All you get it out of it is de-energising negativity.

Does that sound like a deal an exceptional person would sign up to?

Social media has some upsides as it helps you stay connected and can be used to promote your business interests.

And later in this book I will address to how to use social media rather than it using you.

However, you need to take active control and exercise discipline, so you don't get distracted by clickbait designed solely to keep you scrolling.

Let's take a moment to do an audit on the information you are constantly absorbing every day.

Look right now at your news and multiple social media feeds.

Stop and think about the content of the talk radio you listen to on the way to work, the combative approach of 24-hour news broadcasts and the screaming horror of newspaper headlines.

As I explained in Chapter One, visualisation is a powerful tool for programming the mind.

And it has motivating and uplifting effects when you focus on the positive; it has the same destructive power when you are always viewing and hearing negative things.

Just look at your news consumption.

You are continually being fed toxic negativity which is eroding your reserves of positive energy.

Are you for real?   You are wasting time on sensationalised nonsense.

It takes lots of time and energy to consume and listen to all this mainly useless information and other people's opinions.

Time which you could put to better, more productive and ultimately more rewarding use.

This is the time you could be spending with your kids, or asking out the girl of your dreams, or thinking about job promotion or even driving to the beach to watch the sunset.

These things are positive and real. Not negative and fake social media fantasy.

If you want to create and generate positive energy, rethink how to use social media. Ask yourself who is benefiting from your time and attention because you should be utilising those things for your own success.

GET UNPLUGGED

So, how do you stop negativity overload draining your precious energy and clogging up your finely tuned life engine?

Firstly, I don't waste time scrolling through social media.

Secondly, I take a complete phone break for six hours every Sunday.

I lock my phone in a cupboard and organise for somebody else to monitor all my digital communications in case an emergency should arise.

Thirdly, when I am on holiday, I don't use my phone at all. This is a great strategy that I have only recently adopted.

I have found when my eyes are not constantly on a screen I am much less stressed and more engaged with every aspect of the real world, including people and my environment.

I understand that being digitally connective can be essential for doing business but it is important to be aware that it can be a time thief that has the capacity to trap you like a rat on a wheel.

So to test just how dependent you are on social media and how much work you need to do to take control, I advise you start with one week's complete digital detox.

This will be a difficult exercise because social media can be a severe addiction for many people because it's been designed to get you hooked.

Don't look at or engage in any way with social media or news output for seven days.

Switch off your alerts and put your phone down unless it's for important calls or business emails.

Don't use your mobile as your alarm clock as it's too easy to click into social media first thing in the morning when you should be exercising and practising your gratitude.

If you can complete this task, then you have effectively turned off the tap to one of the main sources of negative energy in the world. You should be proud of your achievement for mastering control of the information that flows into your life.

However, if you find this exercise hard or impossible to complete, then you have proved to yourself that social media owns you.

How are you going to become exceptional if you are not in complete control of all of your thoughts and actions?

As I have said before, don't be a tool for someone else's gain.

Get addicted to your own success and not the success of social media billionaires.

You have just bought yourself back hours every week in which to do something productive and life-enhancing that will make you exceptional.

TALK TO YOURSELF – POSITIVELY

Studies into brain patterns have conclusively proved that when we use positive words, it releases endorphins and serotonin, which then flows throughout our body, making us feel good.

Control your words. Words control your world.

But the reverse happens when the words within us and around us are negative.

This is a clinically-proven example of how the power of what you hear influences how you feel and act.

Talk may be said to be cheap, but it's impacting on your mind and body at a cellular level and influencing how you feel and act.

It is not who you are that is holding you back. It is who you think you are.

94

Growing up in Belfast in the 1970s and 80s there was a lot of negative talk all around me.

It was in the politics of government, the interactions on the street and even in our homes.

Expectations were low for the whole society, including my friends and I.

Of course, we absorbed the negativity and then began repeating it in our heads.

We permitted ourselves to fail. We were expected to fail because of the situation we were living in. It became the script and the mantra.

All we heard from our key influencers was the things that we couldn't do or the places we couldn't go.

We were encouraged to be cautious and conservative and keep our heads down below the parapet in case they were literally shot off!

There was a lot of 'No, No, No' and that's the narrative as kids we had programmed into our heads because we were living in a dysfunctional society, not of our making.

The prevailing attitude was that there was no point trying to be anything better because the odds were so stacked against us.

The often repeated phrase I heard growing up was 'Don't get above your station, wee lad'.

Honestly, in the 70s & 80s Belfast success and achievement could make you a target because you were not complying to the script of failure.

No-one was allowed to get above themselves or given space, time or support to challenge their negative destiny.

Times were so bad; parents considered their offspring a success if they simply avoided becoming a member of a paramilitary organisation, going to jail or getting killed!

If you lived in a tough working-class neighbourhood in Belfast, the bar was set pretty low when it came to expected achievement.

Success was not for the likes of us, so we didn't talk about it, and the majority of people never achieved it because they didn't think success was an option.

There was no positive internal or external conversation going on about success, never mind instructions on how to become exceptional.

But even as a young child of 10-years-old, I wanted to hear something different.

I wanted to be someone different.

As I shared with you earlier, I was working in a fish & chip shop, and I was earning money.

At that young age, I already realised that money was a tool that gave me control over my destiny.

I could make my own future rather than just accepting what was being given to me.

I knew through hard work and application success was possible.

That may have been 37 years ago but it still applies today.

It applies to me and it applies to you – anything is possible if you have the right energy and mindset.

MAKE THE CUT

We are all human, and so we all have 'down' days, but how you manage them will have a direct effect on how you react in any given situation.

I will come back to this in more detail in chapter five when we will examine motivation.

You need to have a cheerleader and life coach in your mind to keep you energised at all times.

Some people seem to have down days every day!

You know who they are, and you actually feel them draining your positive energy before you even interact with them.

The truth is the perpetually negative people don't want solutions to their problems, they just want your sympathy.

They have no intention of changing because they are comfortable in their misery.

Cut these perpetually negative people out of your life right now - regardless of who they are – move office.

That might sound very harsh, but the attitude of the people you surround yourself with will affect your attitude.

Run with kings or queens and you become one.

If someone has a negative attitude, they are likely to bring down those around them.

While it may be practically difficult to cut negative family members or co-workers out of your life completely, you must limit your time, exposure and tolerance to these people.

One of the best strengths you can develop is the power to say 'no' to negativity.

The word 'no' is a shield of protection against negative vibes.

That means negativity from any source – pessimistic people, drugs, alcohol, bullies – don't give permission for things that have a bad effect on your alignment to even enter your life.

That way you won't have to waste time getting rid of them.

There's a saying - **'You are the average of the five people you spend the most time with.'**

My advice is to pick wisely when it comes to the people who you let get close to you.

In my professional life, experience has taught me to be the lone wolf.

As humans, we have a tendency to take on the perspectives and outlook of others, so it's important to be with people who have an upbeat mindset and practice positive self-talk.

Spending time with positive people will bring out the best in both you and in them as it multiples the energy.

When you are feeling low, this is the time to do something productive and rewarding and build your self-esteem back up.

Think and act decisively and attend to your business in a motivated way.

Accept the fact that the more you find your true self, the more fake people you will want to lose.

This advice also applies to you. Leave your negative baggage and emotional soap opera dramas at the front door and don't become the energy vampire you are doing your best to avoid.

Check your thoughts and your words and keep them upbeat and professional at all times.

By following my Five Golden Principles of Dream to Achieve, you are already becoming a beacon of positivity that is now attracting success.

Dream big because you are on an amazing journey towards being exceptional.

Positive energisation is the engine that is going to keep you motoring up that steep hill.

Believe in your capabilities.

You will quickly see the difference it makes in your thoughts, words, actions and energy levels.

Even on your darkest down days, you must still go through the motions and I will return to this in more detail later in this book.

GENERATE POSITIVE ENERGY AT ALL TIMES TO BE EXCEPTIONAL AND FULFIL YOUR DREAMS!

<u>Mission Statement</u>

If you can't control your energy, it will prove very difficult to control much of anything in life.

You are the only person who can make this happen.

TOM'S TIPS FOR ENERGISATION

- Control your energy so you can control everything in your life.
- There's a direct connection between the right energy and the right results.
- Always remember that the difference between success and failure is your attitude.
- You have the power to change your perspective through positive energisation.
- You are continually projecting an energy field through your words and actions.
- Positive energy is infectious and your upbeat attitude will transform whomever you are interacting with.
- Your energy sets the agenda for every interaction.
- Smile and say 'yes' more.
- Present the best version of yourself in every way.
- Keep your activity levels high and seek new, positive challenges.
- Research what successful people say and do and then mimic that in your own life.
- Avoid the 'drains' and stay close to the 'radiators'.
- Unplug from social media and avoid the contagion of other peoples' negativity.
- When you are feeling low, do something productive and rewarding.
- Keep your internal and external dialogue positive and full of potential and energy.
- Start and end your day with a positive affirmation.

DREAM

Chapter 4: Ambition

Every single day I feel so blessed and eternally grateful that I have the unlimited ambition to power me through life.

I am entirely confident that I have an exceptional ability to accomplish everything I want because I work hard to achieve my dreams.

I have learned that ambition is the essential quality you need to become an exceptional person who achieves great things.

Ambition is simply defined as 'a strong desire to do something' and having the determination to achieve success.

In this chapter, I am going to share with you my secrets to help you explore, define and then achieve your core ambitions.

I am going to help you break the shackles of small thinking that have been limiting your dreams and holding you back all these years.

You are going to fire up your ambition and take control of your destiny.

You can be ambitious in anything you choose.

ARE YOU AMBITIOUS?

Let's take my ambition quiz to provide some insights into your thinking:

1. Are you prepared to compromise your standards? Are you ready to do whatever it takes to achieve your goals?

2. Do you believe you are a strong and confident leader? Do you think you are the best?

3. Are you prepared to take risks to achieve your goals?

4. Do you always play to win – regardless of what you are doing?

5. Are you curious to get new knowledge and skills? Do you read regularly to better your understanding, and do you work on yourself for constant self-development?

6. Will you make significant sacrifices to attain your goals?

7. Are you focused on process or outcome?

8. Whom do you compete with?

9. Do you think luck plays a key role in your success?

10. Do you take responsibility for your actions?

THE RIGHT ANSWERS

1. Those with high achievement motivation have incredibly high standards and will not compromise. They are prepared to do whatever it takes to succeed. Ambitious people understand that there are no short cuts, and it is only their persistence that will get them what they want.

2. Ambitious people always believe they can lead others, and they want to be at the top of their game. They believe they are the best.

3. People with ambition are always willing to do what it takes to achieve their goals, which may sometimes involve risk and criticism. Ambitious people act with purpose but are flexible and curious.

4. You should not turn your ambition off and on like a tap. You need to apply it to your every action.

5. To be radically ambitious, explore and learn new things each day. Be curious about problems, not defeated by them. Ask questions to get new information and make meaningful connections. Ambitious people break away from consistent groupthink.

6. To be genuinely ambitious, you must accept that input equals output. Ignore distractions and obligations and put everything into your passions.

7. Ambitious people put the main emphasis on pulling the trigger - they get shit done. If your execution is lacking, nothing matters.

8. Your most significant competitor should be yourself. Don't compare yourself with others. Nothing beats hard work with focus and passion. So really stretch yourself mentally, physically and psychologically. As one of the world's great life and business coaches Grant Cardone says: 'Never compete – dominate.'

9. Being successful is all about how badly you want it and how much you're willing to work for it. The only time luck plays a role is when you are in the right place at the right time, but it's up to your ambition to get yourself to the right place. As the Roman philosopher, Seneca said **'Luck is what happens when preparation meets opportunity'**.

10. If you want to be more ambitious, you should cultivate the habit of being intensely self-sufficient and responsible. Exceptional people don't leave stuff up to others; they're going to do it on their own to make sure that it's done on time and in the right way. They accept that the buck stops with them. They take the heat when things go wrong, and they have earned praise when they go right.

After taking my quiz, do you think you are naturally ambitious?

If not, you need to get some fire in your belly right now if you really want to achieve your dreams.

If you don't fundamentally believe you will be successful, you can't persuade anyone else that you will be.

Use my DREAM system every day to cultivate your ambitions and make them a reality.

The definition of 'success' will be unique to each individual. Still, the journey remains the same: it's essential to have goals and the determination to complete them.

Your personal definition of success can be in any or every area of your life. Whether that means being the best business leader, the greatest parent, a prolific author, and elite sportsperson or a world-class entertainer. The choice is yours!

Here are five things ambitious people do:

1. **Become an expert your field** – be the person that dominates that market because they know it inside out.

2. **Physical health** – a healthy mind and healthy body go together. Energy and stamina are required to pursue ambition ruthlessly. Having exceptional physical and mental health is essential if you want to chase down and catch your dreams.

3. **Find new challenges** – Never live in the comfort zone as contentment kills opportunity. The comfort zone is only for the weak.

4. **Productive interpersonal relationships** - ambitious people understand they are only as good as their support network. Treat people with respect but don't allow yourself to be undermined by those who don't respect you.

5. **Having timetabled plans** – keeping ambition on track with goal statements and planning is essential to see results. Planning will optimise productivity. Never have space in your diary – have your day planned from the moment you wake up to the time you go to bed. Your whole-day schedule should be filled with your training, goal statements, business social media posts, phone calls, emails, chasing leads and referrals and spending productive time with your children and family. Time is money! Every minute of your time is valuable so you must monitor how much you are wasting doing nothing or investing doing productive things. Downtime is lost time. If you don't have control of your time, you will end up working to other people's agendas. Your time is your own – manage it in a way that contributes to your success.

The core elements of ambition remain the same, regardless of the goals you are pursuing.

To reach your full potential, you need to get up early every morning with drive and enthusiasm to tackle every task you face, from taking the kids to school after a good breakfast or engaging in high-stakes business negotiations.

Whatever ambition you choose, work hard every day to be the very best you can be.

How you achieve your ambition sets the standards for those around you.

You must set an example of discipline and always striving to be exceptional.

This sets the agenda for those around you – especially your children. If they see that your focus and continual hard work leads to success, they will emulate your actions.

Your behaviour and actions lay down the blueprint for success.

Keep in mind that you show other people how to behave with your actions, so lead by example.

Your mindset should always be 'do as I do' which is much more effective than 'do as I say'.

That's because you are actually showing people what's possible.

Once they see what can be achieved, it inspires them, and you earn their respect.

It also removes their excuse for not trying something because it seems impossible or unreasonable.

This personal story illustrates exactly how you need to think if you are going to be a winner.

Be prepared to lead from the front and set an example to those around you.

Recently, some of my construction crew were tasked to complete a complicated repair to a roof in what was admittedly challenging weather and site conditions.

They didn't want to do the job because they believed it was impossible and feared they could not do it.

They raised their objections directly to me and then gave me a list of reasons why they believed the job couldn't be done.

"OK", I said. "Don't do the job if you think it's impossible and it can't be done. Carry on with the other jobs on the site."

Today, my work gear is a tailored suit, handmade shoes and a Rolex watch – all of which I am eternally grateful for.

But the next day, I turned up at the construction site dressed in my manual work gear and carrying my tools.

I said nothing to the team who was just stood there looking at me in amazement.

I assessed the job, picked up the materials I needed and scaled the ladder to fix the roof.

This was the first time I'd done a roof repair in almost a decade.

And when I got up there, I could see this was a pretty tricky job to stage my comeback!

I had to challenge myself and really dig deep to overcome this challenge.

But I must be honest – it felt amazing to be back on that roof doing the job that set me on the path to success.

It allowed me to reflect on where I started and to be genuinely grateful in the moment for everything I have today.

Feeling the sun on my face and the wind on my neck, I got a real buzz out of the hard graft.

I really appreciated how being on the roof gives you a different perspective on the world.

You need to really focus on the task at hand and block out all distractions and fear.

Working at height gets the adrenalin flowing and the heart racing in a different way to the cut and thrust of the boardroom.

Jeopardy and danger are immediate, but the rewards of seeing a job completed properly when everyone else said it couldn't be done are priceless.

When I descended the ladder, my crew came over and shook my hand. My exceptional effort was worth it to earn my team's respect.

I was able to get them to question their expectations of what is achievable.

They believed the task was impossible, so they didn't even want to try.

But when the challenge is beaten, and the goal is achieved, you can shift the mindset of everyone.

Take, for example, British sprinter Roger Bannister breaking the four-minute mile record in 1954.

Elite athletes had been chasing the goal from 1886, and despite every attempt, no one could do it.

It had become as much a psychological barrier as a physical one because it was universally accepted that it was beyond the limits of the human body.

Up until Bannister ran a mile in 3 minutes 59 seconds, everybody in the world thought it was impossible because it had never been done before.

However, just 46 days after Bannister smashed the record, Australian runner John Landy not only broke the barrier again but he did it in a time of 3 minutes 58 seconds.

Just a year later, three runners in a single race broke the four-minute barrier.

Since then, more than a thousand runners have broken a time barrier that was considered impossible.

This didn't happen because runners suddenly gained superpowers.

What actually evolved was their mindset.

The power of the mind is unlocked when the impossible is achieved.

That is a powerful lesson whether you are an athlete, scientist or entrepreneur.

In their book, The Power of Impossible Thinking, Yoram Wind and Colin Crook devote an entire chapter to an assessment of Bannister's feat.

Their analysis reveals it was a mindset, not a physical achievement that allowed the time barrier to be smashed.

Bannister was the agent of change. His achievement is remembered to this day because he was the first to do it and because he proved an essential truth.

Suppose you are powered by a strong ambition to be exceptional, and you have the determination to smash your personal limitations. In that case, you can achieve what everyone else believes to be impossible.

If someone tells you it can't be done, just remember the same things were said repeatedly to Roger Bannister!

Truly exceptional people don't accept limitations, tradeoffs, and middle-of-the-road ideas.

In other words, exceptional people don't just out-perform their rivals; they define and evolve the idea of what's actually possible.

To be an agent of change and an icon of success, you must present the highest standards of ambition and action in every single thing you do.

You must accept and believe that greatness exists within you, and ambition is the way to release it.

Think about it – other people have Malibu beach houses, performance sports cars, take holidays in five-star destinations and have impressive careers and family life.

So why shouldn't you?

What are they doing to live this incredible life of abundance?

What are you not doing that is holding you back from living the same life as them?

The good news is that it is never too late to be a success because being ambitious is a choice you can make any time.

You need to flip your mental switch and make a choice to be ambitious for your life.

Ambition does not just belong to young people.

Age is no barrier to achieving your dreams.

And here is a finger-licking example to prove my point.

There are probably very few people on the planet who would not instantly recognise the face of Colonel Harland Sanders, the founder of Kentucky Fried Chicken, or KFC as it's now known.

Colonel Saunders is literally the embodiment of a global brand. His image is synonymous with the billion-dollar fried chicken outlet. Still, he did not achieve any level of success until he was in his mid-70s!

And this was only after a long life of hardship, poverty, failure and tragedy.

Born in 1890, his father died when he was just five.

This meant he had to help his mother by cooking for his siblings while she worked two jobs to make ends meet. That's where he learned to cook cheap, fast and delicious food.

When he was in his 40s, he opened a diner and truck stop selling fried chicken, but it was forced to close down after a road bypass took away his passing trade.

His challenges were further compounded when the restaurant burned down - but not before he was involved in a fatal shooting with a competitor. A row sparked because Saunders was painting advertising signs on barns promoting his business, and an investigating official was shot dead by the man who raised the complaint.

This unfortunate incident is proof that Saunders never backed down from a fight, no matter what he was facing.

He genuinely believed he was bullet-proof and tested it in the most literal way! (I'm not recommending you do that!)

Even before he opened his truck stop, Saunders had racked up an impressive string of career failures including being dishonourably discharged from the army, operating a ferry company until a new bridge put him out of business, losing his law license because he got a criminal record for fighting, opening a lamp company but his rivals were selling a better version, working as a mid-wife (yes, really!) and being divorced by his first wife because of lack of success and inability to provide a steady income for his family!

In 1952, aged 62, Saunders was living off a $100 social security cheque when he incorporated Kentucky Fried Chicken and began driving his 1946 Ford around the country personally signing up new franchisees and customers.

It's worth noting that his famous herbs and spices secret recipe was rejected 1,009 times before anyone accepted it.

But ambition drove him on through all his challenges, and eventually, his dream became a reality.

When Saunders died aged 90, there were around 6,000 KFC locations in 48 countries.

By 2013, there were an estimated 18,000 KFC locations in 118 countries.

WOW!

So, if you're ever feeling overwhelmed by rejection or discouraged by setbacks, remember Colonel Sanders' unconquerable spirit.

Sanders believed in himself and his product so much that he just continued to chase his ambitions until he succeeded.

He was born with the ambition to succeed, and he used all the hardships he faced to get experience and develop fortitude in the face of adversity.

Saunders is a perfect example of how ambition is born of passion.

Passion originates from the simple love of doing something and ambition drives your passion towards your goals.

Ambition magically transforms your passion from thought to action.

But don't confuse ambitions with aspirations.

Aspiration involves striving towards a specific goal; whereas ambition is a personality trait that you can be born with or you can develop.

Ambition should be with you all the time as it drives you to create new goals and pursue them with intent.

BELIEVE IN YOURSELF

Your ego is your sense of self-esteem or self-importance.

If you can combine a big ego with ultimate bravery, you will be ambitious.

Bravery lets you pursue grand goals, and ego will convince you that you deserve a better life.

This combination results in extreme ambition, which leads to the extreme actions needed to be an exceptional person.

Be confident in your abilities.

If you totally believe you can reach your goals and get all the things you want, you will become more and more ambitious.

No matter what has happened in the past, know in your own head that you are going to make it. If you can hold that thought at all times, everything that follows will be easy.

Trust the process. You don't need to figure out how it's going happen – leave the process to the Universe.

The critical point is that it doesn't matter when or how you spark your ambition.

It only matters that you pursue it with 100 per cent commitment and complete determination.

Here's my straight-down-the-barrel advice - stop planning and take action now!

Set fire to your fears and commit to being exceptional.

You are fearless.

Say it to yourself and mean it.

Your determination, energy, ambition and motivation combine to give you an unbreakable shield.

If you believe, you will achieve.

My favourite story to illustrate this is UFC champion Conor McGregor's much-anticipated 2017 fight against Jose Aldo at the MGM arena in Las Vegas.

McGregor, a former plumber from Dublin, simply believed he was going to win this fight. He told anyone who would listen in the months and weeks leading up to the bout.

He went out of his way to demean and unsettle his opponent's ambitions before he even stepped into the ring.

The odds were stacked against him. But in the minutes before the fight, there was a genuine sense from his loyal Irish fans in the arena that McGregor was going to win.

Through the Irish fighter demeanour, words and burning ambition, his countrymen were just confident his triumph was inevitable.

His ambition was so strong that he actually projected it into the hearts of those around him.

His intimidating Brazilian opponent, undefeated in 18 bouts since 2005, would be knocked out cold by McGregor in just 13 seconds of the first round.

Yes – you read that right. 13 seconds!

McGregor lived up to his nickname 'Notorious' when he landed a savagely well-timed left-hand punch that sent Aldo instantly to the canvas unconscious.

Stepping out of the ring to celebrate his stunning victory, what McGregor had to say is testament to his supreme confidence and driving ambition. **"No power, just precision, No speed, just timing. That's all it takes."**

The Irish king of combat sport's demeanour was so matter-of-fact because he simply believed he was fulfilling his destiny.

And you must channel the same spirit to achieve your ambitions by believing you have already knocked your opponent out.

You are only one big punch from your destiny of success.

My biggest competitor is myself. I know if I can dominate my own will and smash my goals, I can beat anything and anyone.

Building a healthy level of ambition is not an easy task, especially amidst so much uncertainty.

But it is really worth the effort. Driving ambition leads to creativity, innovation and greater levels of performance.

Ambition is not always a natural skill you are born with, but it can be learned and cultivated.

A lack of ambition can be overcome.

My ambition to succeed in life started when I was a young child.

It has only increased as I have matured.

With every success, my ambition becomes stronger.

The more ambition I have, the more outstanding my achievements.

Ambition is the rocket fuel for your accomplishments.

How much ambition you have will determine how far you go.

So think BIG!

Set goals for yourself that seem impossible. Always look to the higher target so if you aim to make £100 million per year, instead of just £10 million, and you fall short, you will still get £70 million instead of £7 million.

Ask yourself now – what are you prepared to do for success?

Be committed to achieving your ambitions-whatever the cost because you have the power to decide if you are a winner or a loser.

WHAT IS AMBITION?

'**Ambition is the path to success. Persistence is the vehicle you arrive in.**' – Bill Bradley.

Having ambition is not the same as being greedy.

The difference between greed and ambition is that a greedy person wants things they are not prepared to work for.

When you are an ambitious person, you know what you want and have clear goals and how to achieve the goals.

But more importantly, you are ready to work exceptionally hard to achieve the goals.

You embrace challenges because you see them as a force that will make you stronger.

You must waken every day with a burning desire to succeed and improve. Make sure everyone around you knows this.

Here's a funny story that tells you how much ambition I exude. When my daughter was just a little girl, she overheard a conversation I was having with a client on the phone to close a big deal.

When I finished the call, she burst into tears. Naturally concerned, I asked her what was wrong.

She heard me tell the client I was prepared to run through a brick wall to secure his business. My child was genuinely concerned I was going to hurt my head because, even at five years old, she knew her daddy always did what he said he would do!

Having a strong desire to succeed is what drives winners to advance and achieve their goals, regardless of the challenges they face.

Ambition is the energy necessary to chase your goals, whether in the personal, social or professional field.

It's a necessity for those who want to achieve a specific goal, such as becoming a billionaire CEO, a famous movie star, an elite athlete, or a political leader.

Ambition is the desire to achieve something significant - but it needs to be accompanied by persistence, determination, regeneration, energization and motivation.

These qualities combined will drive you towards achieving all your dreams and goals.

Without the desire to win, to grow and to achieve better results, you will stagnate and fail.

It's always the ambitious person's desire for change that leads to lucrative transformations.

Ambition is crucially important because it is the blueprint for desire, which is the most effective motivator of action.

SMASH YOUR LIMITATIONS

Have you ever heard the saying, 'the sky's the limit'?

Well, not in my book!

When you embark on this journey of success with me, you have no limits!

You must commit yourself to reject any limits, even the sky!

The sky may be the limit for other people, but exceptional people want to go into space.

Your self-doubts can only limit your ambitions, so don't determine your potential with a lack of self-confidence.

Sometimes your biggest enemy and ambition destroyer is the one in your head.

If you are the problem, then you are also your own solution.

The number one thing holding you back is fear.

Fear of rejection. Fear of failure. Fear of poverty.

But fear kills ambition.

So ironically, you have more chance of failing if you give in to your fears.

What have you got to lose?

Just take that step to make it happen. Send that important email now, make that urgent call right away, connect with the people and things that will help you to fulfil your potential.

Get shit done!

Fear is myth – it is not real.

Opportunity won't knock your door. You need to go and hunt it down.

As Grant Cardone advises, do not put time and space between yourself and your challenges.

Challenges are like weeds; they don't go away by themselves.

The longer you ignore them, the more they are going to take root and spread.

Its's not long before they get completely out of control.

For example, I don't need to tell you that putting a credit card bill to the bottom of the pile won't make it disappear.

In fact, as it sits ignored, it's probably accruing interest and greater debt.

This simply illustrates how not facing up to your challenges will cost you in the long run.

So take action now by tackling the most challenging task first. Take back control of every area of your life.

What does FEAR stand for when you surrender to it?

Frustration, Ego, Anxiety, Resentment or False Evidence Appearing Real.

What does FEAR stand for when you conquer it?

Face Everything And Receive.

Jack Canfield, one of America's top success and personal fulfilment trainers, once noted: *'Everything you want is on the other side of fear.'*

You need to get over that wall of fear to achieve your goals, no matter how high it is.

Ambition is the quality that will make you soar higher than your greatest fears.

Have goals big enough to smash the small hassles and daily challenges because the end goal is the most important thing.

The process is incredible and it will help you rise above the daily grind.

It's the building blocks of your success.

Learn to love the hustle. Learn to love the struggle.

Embrace the fact that both will be the making of you.

DEMOLISH THE WALLS

Growing up in Belfast, I saw for myself how limiting beliefs destroy ambition and drive.

We were penned in by actual walls, and our limitations literally felt set in stone.

It was the sort of city where it was dangerous to attract the wrong type of attention, so people kept their head down.

In fact, there's a famous Belfast phrase which goes 'whatever you say, say nothing.'

In other words, keep quiet and blend in. Don't get above yourself. Don't get above your station.

Don't put your head above the parapet in case it actually gets shot off!

I even remember my dad, (who is an amazing father and true legend), advising me not to buy a BMW when I was a young man. He was so worried an expensive, flash car might incite jealousy, which would lead to trouble.

I understand that he was only looking out for me in a very paternal way.

Still, it illustrates why you need to have the strength of character and ambition to believe in yourself and reject any limitations – no matter whom they come from or however well-meaning.

Here's how the sparks of ambition ignited in me back in pre-ceasefire Belfast.

As I said, I had been working since I was about 10-years-old, and I knew that having ambition, control, and money were the keys to creating a better future.

I remember at around age 18 talking to my mates in the pub and telling them my ambition was to buy a house as soon as possible.

They literally laughed at me and said I was living in fairytale land - did I think I was Prince Charming?

In tough, working-class Belfast even such a simple ambition was rejected as unachievable.

Which is truly tragic when you see the negative impact The Troubles inflicted on generations of squandered futures.

115

I witnessed many of my friends have their potential squandered because they were denied the right mindset and circumstances to set them up for success.

Their life chances were totally undermined by the politics and violence of the conflict.

Some of them were talented enough to become professional footballers and emulate their sporting hero East Belfast-born George Best.

Others could have done well in business, entertainment or education.

Sadly, many of these young men with raw talent ended up in jail or dead. They were let down and sacrificed by a society focused on violence.

Growing up, we all had real and imaginary walls put up around our ambitions and our dreams.

We were repeatedly told that we were not supposed to enjoy individual success or to have personal ambitions.

In the conflict situation in Belfast in the 1970s and 80s, young men from working-class estates were almost expected, if not forced, to join the paramilitary organisations that controlled their areas.

The political cause was always prioritised over personal success or individual happiness.

If you even said you wanted to be successful to get out of the ghetto, you were marked as a traitor to your community.

When I talked about my dream to buy a house outside my neighbourhood, I was subjected to ridicule and abuse because I had challenged the accepted status quo.

For these young people with limited life chances, buying a house at such a young age was an impossible dream.

They didn't even possess the ambition to imagine that reality. Let alone see an investment opportunity.

But I did.

I ignored their jokes and criticism, and in 1994, I bought my first property in Belfast for £30k.

Then on the 31st August of that year, the seemingly impossible happened. The IRA called a ceasefire.

Our world changed forever, and for the better as the rules of engagement were rewritten.

It was the beginning of the end of a violent campaign that had already stretched into its third decade.

By October that year loyalist paramilitaries had followed suit.

The property market reacted to the peace dividend with skyrocketing house prices.

I sold my first house for over three times what I paid for it and set myself on a path to building a property empire.

The guys from the pub weren't laughing at me then.

That's because exceptional and ambitious people are always criticised by those who have given up on their dreams.

They want you to fail to make themselves feel better.

Sometimes friends and relatives will try to put you off out of concern because they fear you will go beyond your comfort zone and get hurt.

I had to focus and believe in myself and let the Universe deal with the process.

Quickly tripling the profit on my first house not only gave me my financial start, but it also provided a huge psychological boost.

All of a sudden, I clearly understood that my ambitions could be realised if I kept focus and believed in my dreams.

My ambition made me believe in myself, even when nobody else did.

It was a straightforward equation that could be followed if I just had faith in myself and in the Universe to deliver.

If I could repeat the process with more properties, I would continue to build profit.

The end result would be I could own lots of properties and enjoy significant financial return by renting them out.

Bricks and mortar exist in the real world and always make for a solid investment, unlike the non-existent digital capital of stocks and shares.

117

I knew I could build a different life and career for myself.

Where I come from is not important.

It even worked in my favour because struggle and deprivation had made me hungry for success.

Belfast at this time was also hungry for success.

When the opportunity manifested for peace and prosperity, our society came together and worked hard to achieve our ambitions for normality.

The story of Northern Ireland's transformation should inspire you as it proves what can be achieved if you believe and take massive action.

I am so proud of how our society turned its fortunes around, despite the enormous challenges which once seemed impossible to solve.

We have to overcome entrenched thinking and historical hurt to achieve our giant dreams and future ambitions.

Here's what former US president Bill Clinton said in April 1998 about the Northern Ireland Peace Pact: 'The path of peace is never easy. But the parties have made brave decisions. They have chosen hope over hate; The promise of the future over the poison of the past. And in so doing, already they have written a new chapter in the rich history of their island, a chapter of resolute courage that inspires us all.'

Such was our journey of transformation that Northern Ireland has become a model for conflict resolution around the world.

Please let our journey inspire your personal transformation.

This success was really brought home to me a few years ago when I was trying to call a friend without success for over a week.

He had gone 'missing in action' without explanation.

When he did eventually ring me back, I jokingly asked if he had been hiding up a mountain for the last week because nobody could get in touch with him.

I was stunned when said he had actually been in a cave in Afghanistan working with someone he formerly considered an enemy teaching the Taliban fighters and leaders techniques on peaceful conflict resolution!

They had been invited by the EU Ambassador to Afghanistan to share their experiences of how they challenged their thinking to overcome massive obstacles.

As a result of their engagement, the Taliban and Afghan government reopened their negotiations based on the sharing of Northern Ireland's experience of not doing more to help victims after the conflict ended.

When I heard this story, I felt so proud and grateful for just how far our society has come over the last two decades in Northern Ireland.

Such was the personal effort invested that two previously mortal enemies were able to come together to teach peace to others.

This happened only because of individual and collective action and a massive belief in overcoming what seemed impossible for generations.

If that is achievable, then you can do anything.

We managed to tackle a problem that seemed impossible to solve, and one that makes all other issues seem trivial.

But you must be prepared to do whatever it takes and to remain committed to success.

Break the mould and move out of your comfort zone.

Your background is irrelevant as it's not about where you start, but how you play the game and where you finish.

Stop using your past as an excuse for future failure.

In fact, you must use your previous struggles as fuel to push you towards success.

Your ambitions must be greater than your fears if you ever hope to achieve your dreams.

As Grant Cardone says, **'When you learn to look bigger than your original goals and aim for something that seems impossible, you're setting up the framework for success'.**

If you want to fuel your ambition and achieve your dreams, first you need to identify what your goals are and zone in with laser focus.

By identifying goals, creating schedules to achieve those goals and staying committed to that plan, you will fulfil all of your dreams.

What is holding you back? The past? The present? Or even the future? Or is it fear?

CAN'T STOP, WON'T STOP

You need to be a juggernaut - an unstoppable, intimidating, determined, fearless and powerful force of nature.

And that means sometimes you need to be merciless because you must put your end goal first.

Repeat after me – **'Giving up isn't even an option.'**

Persistence of ambitions and actions is the only way to be exceptional.

If you want to be genuinely ambitious and successful, never lower your target; increase your actions.

Remember, in the last chapter; we discussed how massive actions deliver massive results?

Well, ambition is the fuel to power those actions which will drive you on to achieve extraordinary results.

I never feel physically tired because I have created within me a giant spirit of enthusiasm for my life.

That is why I literally jump out of bed every morning at 4am because I can't wait to get to the riches and success every day is going to deliver.

Remember every day is a true blessing and it's up to you to make the most of it.

Life is what YOU make it so make it the best it can be.

It's why I have the stamina to keep working late because I am so excited by the potential in my life that I don't set my projects down. I just get shit done,

You need to have a dream for it to come true, and you must be willing to do whatever it takes to make it happen.

The real key to success is not just thinking big – it's thinking MASSIVE!!!

Again, I take my inspiration for giant thinking from Belfast's two iconic cranes that dominate the city skyline.

And giant thinking is what you need if you are going to become exceptional in life.

No great success ever happened with small thinking.

One of my other great inspirations is Tony Robbins.

He is one of the most successful performance coaches in the world, and he titled one of his books 'Awaken the Giant Within' to highlight the need to think and act big.

He believes we all have the potential to achieve great things. But too often it is an untapped resource that we forget is there or just don't know how to get to it.

Now you know this, you must awaken the giant sense of ambition within you.

Your dreams are your ambitions with a proper plan behind them.

Robbins says 'If you talk about it – it's a dream. If you envisage it, it's a possibility. But if you schedule it, it's real.'

So put a deadline on it with an exact date. Don't be vague because dates bring deadlines, and that brings focus and results.

So make your goals real by working to a schedule to achieve them today.

Everybody has dreams, but only a few exceptional people realise their giant ambitions.

Suppose you don't have a plan and a system in place to achieve massive results. In that case, it's too easy to be distracted by trivial issues and other people's problems.

You need to work at your DREAM system every single day.

It should not be something you dip into, but rather your new way of being in the world.

Remember that crash diets don't work, but a change in attitude toward your diet will help you get healthy.

121

The same applies to personal coaching.

Here are 10 quick ways to help you achieve your ambitions:

1. Have massive goals that genuinely scare you and record your goal statements daily. Monitor your progress and keep track of your goals.

2. Get it done – stop procrastinating and take massive action all the time.

3. Check your alignment every day and make sure you are tuned to the right frequency.

4. Be consistent in everything that you do.

5. Be persistent in everything that you do.

6. Never give up and never take no for an answer.

7. Break your significant challenges down into manageable tasks. For example – if you want to earn a million pounds in a year, that's less than £20,000 per week. If you are in the gym and you don't want to do 20 reps, trick your mind by doing 4 sets of 5 reps instead.

8. Accept failure is all part of the process and learn from your mistakes. You need to fail to move forward.

9. Express your ambitions out loud and make them real. Tell people and talk about them - The Universe will answer, so don't keep your goals a secret.

10. It's all about the end result so remain laser-focused on your goal.

TAKE ACTION TO SUCCEED

Whatever you are concentrating on you, you will become.

As Tony Robbins says: **'Where focus goes, energy flows.'**

This is why it is critical to set firm goals to realise your ambitions.

Once you commit yourself to action through goal setting, you are more likely to follow through on your plans.

Using my DREAM system, I am training you in the tried-and-tested methods that I use every day to achieve my goals.

I am giving you the skills to succeed, but only you know what you want to achieve.

Let me share with you an important lesson. One of the most useful things I have learned on my journey of success is the hugely effective power of a written goal statement.

Once you put pen to paper, you are making a real commitment to yourself and signing a written contract with the Universe to make it happen.

When you are writing your goal statements, you must really focus on every word and let the Universe lead your pen.

Visualise yourself achieving these goals and how success will transform your life for the better.

You are the lead character in your life, so give yourself heroic and epic challenges and goals.

So I now want you to take a minute to really focus on your goals.

The Universe loves lots of detail when you are writing your goal statements and ambitions.

You must clearly state what you want to get out of life.

Make your dreams massive and then take giant actions to achieve them.

Imagine what your life would be like if all those dreams become your new reality.

Think about how fulfilling your goals will make you feel.

Get a journal and write down your top five goals every single day, so they are real and exist out in the world.

Beside them write down a precisely dated deadline for achieving them.

Write your goal statements down first thing in the morning before you start your day, and you are already ahead of the game.

This will help you focus on the thoughts and actions required to achieve all of your huge goals.

Decide what you need to do daily to make your goals happen. Plan what you need to do, what calls you need to make, what emails you have to send, what meetings you have to go to or site visits you must make.

Write it down and take massive action to make it happen.

I don't expect my destiny just to turn up; I always take massive actions to get massive results.

You must fully commit to believing that nothing you can dream is impossible to achieve.

Goals give you focus. Focus creates momentum for action.

Ambition may be the first rung of the ladder of success, but the second step is action.

To reach the top quicker, you need to take massive action.

Think carefully about what has held you back and stopped you taking action to make your dreams a reality.

Don't be held back by past mistakes and don't waste your energy on regret.

Use previous challenges to help you avoid future mistakes.

Take time to regularly assess where you are on the path of your journey to success.

You must always be honest with yourself. If you feel you are underperforming, then make an immediate and effective adjustment to your thinking and behaviour to get back on track.

I had to do a reality check recently. I was putting too much of my energy into babysitting my sales team in one business and neglecting the proactive actions needed for my other companies' development.

I was distracted from the bigger picture and wasn't investing the time I needed to achieve my more significant goals.

I had to check my current co-ordinates on my journey map and reset my course of action to get back on track.

Luckily, I was self-aware enough to notice that I had been blown off course by badly-managed energy.

So always be mindful that you are using your energy in the right places.

Make detailed notes about how and when you are going to achieve your goals. Make sure you are doing some activity every day that moves you closer to achieving them.

For example, I consider all of my businesses like burning fires that I must tend and keep alight.

That means I must give equal attention to each and add fuel to them when needed to stop them from extinguishing.

It is my job as chief fire tender to monitor and manage the fires. I need to know when it's time to pour petrol on a particular fire to create a huge blaze or simply keep it burning consistently.

Or when to stoke them with more wood if the energy in them is falling.

I use this metaphor in my head to keep me focused on the task of keeping all my business fires burning equally and all producing massive heat.

I apply the same theory to my personal relationships.

EVERYTHING IS POSSIBLE

You must fully commit to believing that nothing you can dream is impossible to achieve.

You must feel that everything is possible.

Share your ambitions with the Universe in a committed way, so it knows what you need and want.

It's as simple as ordering your favourite takeaway burger.

Goals are like placing your order from the Universe.

When you place your order, trust the process and the Universe will deliver it.

So be clear and concise about what you want. The Universe can't give you a deluxe Big Mac if you keep ordering a McMuffin!

Five Goal-Setting Tips

1. **Be Specific** – your goal must be well defined.

2. **Have a timetable** – give yourself a confirmed and dated deadline to achieve your goal.

3. **What's your motivation** – understand why your goal is essential to you.

4. **Have a plan** – write down and display your goals, so that you are reminded to work towards them daily. Get it done!

5. **See it** – achieve your goals faster by visualising your success.

You need to cultivate ambitions and dreams so big that they simply overshadow any problems or challenges in the way of achieving them.

When it comes to sales motivation and helping people really develop their ambitions, billionaire business coach Grant Cardone is unbeatable.

He is the bestselling author, sales trainer, speaker, and entrepreneur who has worked in real estate and the auto industry. He is a real estate mogul who built his $1.5 billion portfolio properties from scratch, and he was named number one marketer by Forbes Magazine.

I really respect how he does business, his mindset, experience and drive.

I admire how he helps others achieve their dreams, so when he says the quote below, I believe everyone who dreams of being exceptional needs to take note.

'The single biggest financial mistake I've made was not thinking big enough. I encourage you to go for more than a million. There is no shortage of money on this planet, only a shortage of people thinking big enough.'– Grant Cardone.

Grant is adamant that if you're just working hard to be comfortable, then the bad news is you're going to be working forever.

You will never achieve your goals because comfort means complacency.

Your goal should be freedom, not comfort.

Take, for example, the attitude to success of Reed Hastings, the CEO of Netflix which is the world's biggest streaming service.

"We suck. We're pretty good. But we suck, compared with how we're going to be in three years."

Despite already being the boss of a $230bn (£175bn) entertainment colossus, Hastings' desire to improve and innovate never stops.

He can't stop because he's propelled by an ambition to be exceptional and he takes massive action to stay ahead of the competition.

And if you want to emulate that success, you need a supreme level of commitment.

There is no Plan B.

There's only Plan A – A for ambition!

Here's why;

If you have a Plan B or an exit strategy, then you are planning for failure.

You are telling the Universe that your plan A has the potential to fail.

Imagine the scenario of a tightrope walker stepping out on to the wire hundreds of feet above the ground without the aid of a safety net.

The tightrope walker can only do this because they have 100 per cent faith Plan A won't fail.

They most believe the rope won't snap, that they won't lose focus or balance and that they can make it to safety on the other side.

The tightrope walker risks everything to simply prove they have more faith and focus than most other people.

You need to have the same attitude to succeed in life.

Elite bodybuilder, movie star and politician Arnold Schwarzenegger said it best: **'I hate plan B. If you can have a plan 'B', then you can never truly focus on plan A, and that's a big mistake. Forget plan 'B'. To test yourself and grow, you have to operate without a safety net.'**

Ambitious people don't accept limits, and they don't let fear hold them back.

They don't wait to have a safety net installed.

They step out with confidence onto that tightrope wire, and they just go for it.

They only see the end goal, and they risk everything to achieve it.

I use fear to help drive me through because it produces adrenaline and action.

The hardest step on any journey is the first one, but once you take it, you will be on your way.

Harnessing fear will help you relax and take more chances which will open more doors to let success in.

PUT A ROCKET UNDER IT!

I personally developed my DREAM system because I have enough positive energy to help many people launch their life on to a higher level of happiness.

I have researched and studied many techniques and read books by some of the greatest and most successful people on the planet.

I have surrounded myself with the right team to help me be exceptional.

I want to share my experiences and learning with you so that you can become exceptional.

That's why I now want to give you one of the greatest exercises ever for launching your life into a higher orbit.

Prepare for take-off!

To turbo-boost your ambition, I'm going to share one of my favourite visualisation exercises that I do with my incredible business coach Daniel Konieczny.

This might seem strange, and you may even be a bit embarrassed the first time you do it, but honestly, this really works. Trust the process and believe in the extraordinary power within you to visualise and then materialise your goals.

This is called the rocket technique, and I am going to talk you through how I do it, and then you need to try it for yourself.

Well now is the time to stand up and try this exercise for yourself.

When I do the rocket technique, first I stand up, close my eyes and visualise something that I am not happy with.

This could be a limiting thought, negative energy, self-doubt, conflict with another person, a deal that hasn't worked out yet - anything that is causing stress, anger or disappointment.

Physically, using my hands and arms, I project that negative problem out and up 10 meters, 100 meters, 1000 meters and then way up into the sky where it explodes in the sun and dissolves.

It's gone. I have let it go, and it no longer has any power or influence on me.

Next, I imagine a huge screen, and I wipe it clean with my gratitude.

I mindfully give thanks for everything I am and everything I have achieved.

I then step forward and clear my energy for the next challenges.

Next, I move into 'Super Tom' rocket launch stage.

This is about visualising my next ambition.

Still with my eyes closed, I see myself going through all of the motions for my next project - such as opening a building of new serviced apartments in a new city.

I achieve this by doing a detailed walk-through in my mind of how this will happen.

When you are doing this process, you need to really see, feel and experience every detail as if it is really happening.

I visualise the reality and immerse myself in the sights, the sounds and even the smells.

You need to imagine every small detail to make it real.

I live the experience in my mind and connect with the vibrations of the Universe to draw power for the next stage of the rocket process.

Daniel then guides me to the 'Super, Super Tom' stage.

I see myself sitting on my new superyacht in the glorious sunshine of the Mediterranean.

My PA, Jacqui, is wearing a white dress and as she walks over to speak to me. She is smiling.

I ask her to wait for a moment. I'm telling a funny story to my friends and family who are sitting on my boat and enjoying my hospitality.

They are laughing and smiling.

These images are so real and detailed I can see and feel the clothes I am wearing – it's a crisp white shirt, pale blue trousers and I have a Mont Blanc pen in my hand.

As I finish my story, I turn to my PA, and she asks me six questions which I answer.

Jacqui tells me that my latest £50 million deal has completed when I sign this document, and as she walks away, I can hear her high heels clicking on the wooden deck of the yacht.

I can feel the sun on my face, smell the suntan lotion and even hear the lapping of the waves against the hull.

I order drinks for everyone to celebrate my latest success.

We open six bottles of the best champagne to celebrate.

So intense is my visualisation, that I can actually taste that champagne! I feel the sensation of happiness flow through my veins.

For some people, this level might be enough. But I want to go further.

So Daniel then confidently and energetically guides me to 'Super, Super, Super Tom' stage.

I visualise myself in the penthouse office overlooking Singapore. I am watching the sun dipping down behind the far horizon, and I am in awe of the beauty of the sunset.

I'm filled from head to toe with gratitude, and I feel the power of realising my dreams.

I am wearing a tailor-made suit and a new diamond-studded Rolex, and I have just made a colossal property deal in Asia.

I know I am a master developer – named one of the best in the United Kingdom – and I have also just struck an incredible deal to sell 50 per cent of my company.

I'm actually living my ambitions in my mind and making then a reality.

Then Daniel slowly counts me down from five to zero. I open my eyes, and utterly I'm buzzing.

We high five each other!!

I'm vibrating with positive energy that's so massive that it fills the room.

I have not just seen my dreams, I have lived every detail of them in my mind.

I trust the Universe to deliver because it never fails - it does not know how to.

I've lived it. It's already happened. The Universe now knows what I expect it to deliver.

Why is this exercise so important, you may ask?

Because you have seen yourself go through an incredible transformation of ambition.

You have lived it and laid down plans for its manifestation.

The Universe does not know it isn't real – yet.

With your thoughts, the Universe can only do one thing - deliver.

It will respond and deliver as though your thoughts have already happened.

Incredible things will start to happen for you when you successfully visualise your ambitions.

It's a fantastic trip when you physically step into a whole new version of yourself and your incredibly successful future.

The rocket visualisation is the fuel that speeds up your journey to achieving your goals.

Incredible things will start to happen when you visualise your ambition no matter what that might be.

To let you into something personal, I know this process works because I carried out a visualisation a year ago and the scenario I ordered from the Universe recently came true.

With my eyes closed as I paced the room, I visualised myself in Belfast city centre. I am wearing a navy pin-striped suit, getting out of my new sports car and going into an office to secure a vast property deal.

131

That very scenario I manifested during my session with Daniel came true exactly as I had pictured it.

I have just moved into the new city centre offices that I pictured in my mind.

The desks are already set up for my new sales team, and the board room is magnificent.

My new car arrived this week, and I'm living out the scene that I put on my vision board and in my visualisation exercises at the start of the year.

I wrote the advance script, took massive actions and the Universe delivered exactly what I had visualised.

Whatever you are thinking about, talking about and are passionate about is more likely to manifest into your life because you are inviting it in.

Remember that whatever you focus on is what you will become.

Try it for yourself and watch how each of your ambitions materialise into reality.

Start with something small as I know it can blow your mind but trust me – if you trust the process, you will produce results so much quicker.

Take the much-loved story of Aladdin.

This tale has been around for thousands of years. It originally appeared in 'A Thousand and One Nights'. This is a centuries-old collection of Arabian stories which were popular long before Disney repackaged them for the modern generation.

Aladdin's story has endured for centuries because it contains a central truth about the power of magical thinking and trusting the Universe to deliver on your dreams.

Now let me tell you the truth about this classic story. It will help you understand the power you already have within you.

When I talk about the magic of Aladdin and the lamp, I am not referring to the magic of Disney. I am talking about the supreme magic of your mind.

OK – let's go through this story and investigate what its symbols really mean.

At the start of the original story, Aladdin's father, Mustapha, dies of shame because of the disappointment he feels about his son's lack of ambition!

Lazy Aladdin's only dream is to marry the beautiful princess.

He didn't want to work for success and believed he could take a short cut to the top.

As the story develops, we begin to understand that it's not just about a lazy guy who finds a magic lamp.

It's actually about the internal magic we all need to tap into for transformative changes.

With this in mind, really think about the elements of this classic story: The Cave, Aladdin, the Lamp and the genie that appears when the lamp is rubbed.

This is a story full of symbols.

Aladdin represents every person who seeks a better life.

The cave where the magic lamp is found stands for your subconscious mind.

The lamp represents the superhuman quality for transformation within the subconscious mind.

Aladdin is tasked with retrieving the magic lamp from this hidden place where it has been forgotten.

This symbol of light represents your superhuman mind and your higher consciousness.

This is where your miracles are formed, but you need the ambition to manifest them into reality.

You must believe in your dream so much that you actually manifest it into reality with hard work and dedication.

Everyday remember to practice – Determination + Regeneration + Energization + Ambition + Motivation = DREAM

In the modern fairytale, Aladdin is granted just three wishes, but in the original ancient version, he has unlimited requests while he owns the lamp.

This is also true for you and confirms that you can ask the Universe for unlimited wishes because you are tapping into the magic of your subconscious mind.

Try it for yourself. Start asking the Universe for small things like a parking space and work your way up to your bigger dreams like getting a new house.

The Universe cannot fail because it doesn't know how to. So trust the process and rub your own magic lamp.

If the lamp is a metaphor for your talent and abilities, are you making the most of YOUR magic lamp?

If you awaken the genie of your ambition, you will have all your wishes granted.

MENTORS OPEN DOORS

My advice is never to be the smartest person in the room.

Be confident enough to lead, but humble enough to seek help and advice when you need it.

It is essential to reach out to the right people for support to help you achieve your ambitions.

Get the right mentor to help you achieve your ambitions as you will learn valuable lessons and be further motivated by their support.

But what is a mentor?

A mentor should be someone who has already surpassed your entrepreneurial goal and a trusted person you feel confident seeking advice from.

A mentor should serve as someone who can teach you, advise you, and pass on their experience.

Modern technology and the internet means we have fantastic access to finding mentors and coaches online.

High achievers share their tips and secrets in books, blogs, videos, podcasts and even personal coaching.

Do your research and arm yourself with insightful information into which mentors' styles work best for you.

Set a target and write it in your goal statements to read, watch and listen to as many of the top-class mentors you can find online.

Make notes as you go about the tips, advice and guidance that personally resonates with you.

You can shop around and find the right guide for the challenges you are facing.

They are teachers, not gurus, so you don't have to stick to just one school of thought.

Ensure you pick the right tool for the right job.

Personally, I would recommend Tony Robbins, Jack Canfield and Gary Vaynerchuk as good starting points.

When I have the opportunity (which I will in the future), I will definitely choose Grant Cardone as my ultimate personal mentor.

He has had a huge positive influence in my life, and I am grateful for all he has taught me.

I believe so much in his methods and teachings that I enrolled all of my sales team at The Grant Cardone Sales Training University for advanced training. This experience has taken both my business and my individual employees to a whole a new level of success.

He is a genuine, motivational sales coach who speaks openly, truthfully and directly.

Grant is the ultimate businessman. I admire him because I understand the challenges and struggles he has overcome in his early life and the amount of work he has put in to become the enormous success he is today.

He has pulled himself up from a working-class background; he has overcome his addictions to drugs and alcohol and refocused his energy into achieving positive life goals.

Grant Cardone is an admirable extremist in that he gives and accepts nothing less than 100 per cent effort multiplied tenfold every single day.

People might think he is an overnight success, but it has taken him more than 20 years of consistent hard work and bravery to get to the top.

He has sculpted himself into becoming one of the great sales team motivators in the world. His wisdom and experience have earned both him and his investors huge dividends.

In 2020, at age 61, Grant Cardone's net worth figure was a reported $300 million, he heads up a massive property empire and offers elite coaching to the world's best executives.

He has sold millions of books, is an internet sensation and he has an army of devoted followers across the world.

He has unquestionably proved the power of hard work and a killer ambition to succeed.

You have to admire his ambitions and dedication. This is why I listen when he gives advice.

Research has shown that having a good mentor is vital to success.

A study of New York tech companies conducted by Endeavor confirms the importance of having a mentor.

It revealed that the 'entrepreneurs leading these startups had strong personal connections to the founders of other successful companies.'

For example, when the Apple founder Steve Jobs passed away, Mark Zuckerberg said that he had been an irreplaceable mentor.

It's good to learn from your own mistakes, but even better to learn from the mistakes of others.

A good mentor will provide you with the following:

• Experienced advice

• A sounding board of advice

• A clear indication of do and don'ts

• An honest account of your performance

• Connections and networking opportunities

• Practical guidance and reassurance

• Encouragement and positivity

• A different insight into your challenges

•Skills improvement through training

You must establish a relationship with a mentor who has your best interests at heart and who also has the right experience and energy level to guide you down the path of success.

Only take advice from someone who is impressive and is smashing life themselves. Ignore and avoid pompous fools and bar-room lawyers.

Inspirational entrepreneur and television host Oprah Winfrey says: '**A mentor is someone who allows you to see the hope inside yourself.**'

By following my Five Golden Principles of Dream to Achieve, you are already developing your core ambitions and setting targets to ensure you achieve them.

AMBITION IS THE DRIVING FORCE THAT WILL PROPEL YOU TOWARDS YOUR DREAMS!

Mission Statement

Vision lets you see where you want to go, and ambition will make you take that journey.

You are the only person who can make this happen.

TOM'S TIPS FOR AMBITION

- Define your goals in detail daily and write them down with accuracy.
- Have a timetable for your success by setting firm deadlines. Deadlines create action and conclusions.
- Forget plan B.
- Identify and overcome your fears.
- Think that big that it seems unachievable.
- Take massive actions all the time.
- Giving up isn't an option.
- Learn from your challenges.
- Truly believe you are going to achieve your goals.
- Trust the process. You don't need to figure out how you are going to do it – trust the mighty universe to deliver.
- Be grateful every day that you can pursue your goals.
- Honour your word.
- Act with confidence.
- Get a mentor.
- Be prepared to do whatever it takes to achieve your goal.
- Take responsibility for your goals and actions.

DREAM

Chapter 5: Motivation

Every morning as soon as I wake, I give sincere thanks for my extreme levels of motivation.

It's the driving force that makes me spring out of bed to embrace whatever challenges I face.

Gone are the days when I used to listen to that voice that says 'hit the snooze button and have a lie-in'.

I can't wait to get up and at the day because I know I am going to be a winner.

Remember, success is a journey, not a destination, so every productive minute of your day counts.

Every step has the potential for progress.

Motivation beats temptation.

It's the driving force that keeps you going.

For massive results, you need to take massive action.

So massive motivation is crucial for setting and attaining your objectives.

Motivation starts with having dedicated daily rituals which you are totally committed to.

If you have something fixed in your timetable, you are less likely to be distracted.

For example, every morning, I get up before the sun at 4am.

Before I am even awake, I know exactly what I am going to do. I'm already feeling motivated.

I now have time and peace to really focus on objectives and properly visualise successful outcomes for all of them.

I get a hit of double (sometimes triple) espresso, check my alignment, write my goal statements and practice my gratitude.

That's my mind up and motivated, and my body will soon follow.

Next, I complete a high-intensity cardio session in the gym to get the blood and endorphins flowing.

I then get to the office before everyone else arrives to get ahead of my work and set a strong example to my staff.

I'm both physically and mentally ready to tackle every challenge the day brings before most other people are even out of bed.

I'm already ahead of the game and radiating with positivity before most people are even awake.

I often hit the gym three times a day, twice before 9am, because it lifts my levels of mental and physical motivation so much.

It's impossible to feel demotivated when you have post-exercise endorphins rushing through your body.

What's driving me is a Lamborghini engine of energy - powered by the rocket-fuel of motivation.

And, that's the level of motivation you need to generate every day if you want to get a serious amount of shit done.

Find out what motivates you. Is it money, fame, excellence or a desire to have power over your destiny?

My Dream system will help you harness the incredible power you have in your mind to achieve precisely whatever you want.

LIVE ON YOUR WITS

Ever since I was I a young child, I have felt a force of motivation driving me onwards and upwards.

In fact, my attitude was so different to everyone around me when I was younger my mother would often joke with me – "You are so driven, sometimes I don't know where we got you!"

Even as a kid, I had a burning desire to have the good things in life.

I wanted to earn my security and my freedom. I wanted to own it so nobody could come and take it away.

But in Belfast back in the 80s and 90s, you had to live on your wits.

At 10 years old, I hustled to get my first job in a fish & chip shop, and I have hustled every single day since.

I will continue to do so forever because I understand the need for energy and consistency.

As a child, I woke up every day with a burning desire to succeed – I can't define it, but it lives inside me every single moment of every day.

Although back then, I didn't understand the complexities of what was driving me. I could see that motivation underpinned by determination will get you almost anything in life.

I learned quickly that if you are motivated enough to put more graft in than anyone else, the rewards will be yours.

There are plenty of people who have more natural talent, ability, intellect and even education.

But there's nobody who is ever going to beat my level of motivation and work ethic.

I use the WIT system in everything I do.

WIT stands for **Whatever It Takes**! I am going to explain the process to attain this mindset in my next book which will be published in Summer 2021.

Live on your wits and be prepared to do whatever it takes to complete a project. You must be motivated enough to do whatever you need to succeed in your goals.

No obstacle should be considered too big to be conquered.

Even if that means walking 500 miles, sending a thousand emails or taking four different flights in 24 hours, I am going to do it whatever it takes to achieve my goals.

My companies are growing from strength to strength because I insist on the same levels of motivation from my staff and management teams.

There is no space in my world for words like 'tried' or 'I did my best' when it comes to completing a task.

Sorry, but in my opinion, that is just another way of saying you failed to do what was necessary.

As I have emphasised, you must change your words to change your world.

Don't accept the vocabulary of failure and stop using it yourself.

Through a lack of motivation, you are just giving yourself excuses to stop trying.

If you are driven by passion, your tasks will never seem like hard work.

For example, if you were told that there's a million pounds in cash waiting for you on the top floor of a skyscraper but the all the lifts are out of order, I bet you would climb every stair without complaining.

On the way up, of course, you will get tired, and out of breath and your muscles will hurt, but you will keep going because you are only thinking about the prize waiting at the top.

That's your motivation driving you.

When you pick up the money, you won't even remember climbing the stairs to get it.

Get focused on the bigger picture. Embrace the journey that gets you to the end goal.

Ability is what you are capable of.

Attitude determines how well you do it.

But motivation is what drives you in the first place.

'The difference between a successful person and others is not a lack of strength, not a lack of knowledge, but rather a lack of will.'- Vince Lombardi.

Motivation is about how bad you want something – if you don't desire success enough, then set this book down right now and don't read any further.

Wanting something is not enough. You must hunger for it and desire it above everything else.

142

Your motivation must be extreme if you are going to overcome the inevitable challenges that stand between you and reward.

Ask yourself: How bad do you actually want it? Will you do it what it takes to achieve your goals?

You must always be hungry for success and prepared to work hard for it.

Accept the fact that if you want a dream life you need to build it because you can't just buy it.

You need to cultivate daily motivation and apply consistency in all elements of your life.

Remember, when you see a man proudly planting a flag on the summit of a mountain, he didn't fall there from the sky.

He first dreamed about standing there, then he made a plan to achieve his ambition and then, through sheer physical effort, he cut a path to the top.

His motivation is what kept him putting one foot in front of the other until he reached his goal.

The mountain climber wasn't pushed by his problems; instead, he was driven by his dreams.

KEEP HUSTLING

Motivation actually keeps us alive because it starts with the basics needed to survive, such as food, water and shelter.

Your next level of motivation is driven by more advanced personal needs such as money, status, power, love, personal fulfilment and self-esteem.

Everybody has some level of motivation from the basic needs of food and shelter, right up to the desire for intellectual, social and physical self-improvement.

Sometimes you are motivated by outside factors and other times your personal internal desires will drive you.

You are only human, and at times your motivation levels will be low, and you will need to dig deep to push yourself on. (I will discuss this in more detail later in this chapter).

At its most extreme, it's often only when you hit rock bottom that you realise you have a reserve tank of ambition and motivation to make you bounce back up.

Success is a lifestyle choice.

Often, you are pursuing your goals for several different motivating factors.

Whatever is driving you, remember you never own success, you just rent it, and you need to pay every day or face eviction.

That should be your core motivation to pursue your goals and ambitions relentlessly.

Research has revealed that we all can influence our own levels of motivation, and in this chapter, I am going to help you with that.

That also applies when it comes to demotivation.

That's your biggest enemy to success.

In the same way that you can be motivated by your ambitions and goals, it is very easy to become quickly demotivated by external distractions.

We all have a million stupid excuses not to do something because we don't feel comfortable asking for it or we are too lazy to get up and do it.

We miss opportunities and fail to get the job done.

Often we expend more energy finding excuses not to do something than it would take to have just done the task in the first place!

Here's my advice – winners don't seek out excuses; they find solutions because they are so strongly motivated to succeed.

They put in at least 10 times more effort than everyone else, and they are driven to take massive actions.

You must push yourself because no-one is going to do it for you.

The dream is free but the hustle is sold separately and that is what you need to pick up the bill for.

Don't wait for good things to happen – go out and make them happen.

'Good things happen to those who hustle.' - Anais Nin

Action always beats intention. Like the mountaineer climbing to the summit, paths must be cut and not just thought about.

Falling back on pathetic justifications not to complete a task that will bring you closer to your goals is a real sign of weakness.

Tough times don't last, but tough people do.

So build up your personal resilience. Never be satisfied with your actions until you are proud of your efforts.

Your best must always be better than everyone else, so set high standards for yourself and everyone around you.

Always be aware of your levels of motivation.

When you feel smug about your success, and you then rest on your laurels, you risk falling into the trap of procrastination and complacency.

Stay hustling and hungry for more – even if I had £50 billion in the bank, I am always going to hustle because I want to be the best version of myself every day.

You need to be stronger, tougher and smarter than any excuses your self-limiting mind comes up with.

Be motivated by the fear of just being average.

Don't be frightened to be different. Instead, you should fear just being the same as everyone else!

'How dare you settle for less when the world has made it so easy for you to be remarkable?'- Seth Godin

That's why your vision board, goal statements and gratitude practice are all so important.

Depending on multiple factors, you won't always be super motivated every day, so that's why you must learn to be disciplined.

This starts with your daily rituals.

I recommend you start your day with physical exercise as its effects will instantaneously improve your levels of motivation for every task you face.

Even though I have such a high level of focus and motivation, I still get those limiting thoughts in my head sometimes.

We all have a disciplined angel on one shoulder and a tempting devil on the other.

Sometimes when I am working out in the gym, my devil of laziness will whisper in my ear to just do 20 minutes on the stair climber machine instead of half an hour.

When this happens, I am ready to counteract it. I push the accelerator pedal of motivation and speed away from my self-limiting thoughts.

I punch that lazy devil in the face and knock it out.

I can do this because I am aware of how easy it can be to get distracted and led off the path of success by sheer laziness.

I'm 100 per cent confident that I always have more in the tank to give.

I drown out the voice temptation to be lazy by turning up the volume of gratitude I'm calling out in my head, and I take my exercise up a few notches instead of giving in.

Why? Because short cuts don't appeal to me.

If you permit yourself to take short cuts in one aspect of your life, you are more likely to do the same in the boardroom, and that is a huge mistake.

Short cuts will end up costing money, destroying your reputation and can even put lives at risk.

Focus on your goal and complete the process correctly so you can enjoy 100 per cent personal confidence in what you are doing.

Winners and champions don't take short cuts and you shouldn't either.

Never stop challenging yourself. The day you do, you're falling behind.

There are no shortcuts to success.

If it doesn't challenge you, it won't change you!

You need vision, hard work and determination to reach the top.

DO IT NOW!!

Make that call, send that email, write that contract now. If you don't, these tasks will keep churning in the background and draining your energy.

Unfinished tasks distract and block your real genius thinking and rewarding actions.

Motivate yourself to be a doer in a world full of people who give up and never finish anything.

Watch the difference in your life when you do stuff immediately and when other people realise that you are super sharp.

When you are keen, willing and able to solve problems and keep hustling, good people will want to work and collaborate with you.

Your reputation as a person who gets things down will motivate not just you but those around you.

You won't be able to build that reputation on what you are going to do but only what you have done.

Personal development coach Gary Vaynerchuk says: **'Work ten times harder and don't be afraid of disappointment. Stop thinking about taking a break because breaks don't get things done. And when you feel like quitting, push your limits a bit further. You'll walk yourself through hell, but in the end you'll know what heaven feels like.'**

As I have explained, I get up every morning at 4am and use the quiet time to set myself up for the day.

I often send emails to clients and contacts during the early morning hours, and often they will comment about the time they get them. They ask me – 'were you not sleeping well, Tom? I saw you were up working in the middle of the night?'

I laugh and say 'no – I sleep brilliantly. What is your middle of the night is actually the start of my day.'

147

Sometimes they are shocked by this response, but I explain that this is my normal.

They know now how seriously dedicated to success I am and it gives them great confidence working with me.

When I say to make that call, I mean really make it.

Keep pursuing your lead until you get a connection.

If they don't pick up the phone, email them. If they don't respond, find them on social media and connect.

If needs be, send a carrier pigeon – whatever it takes.

Do whatever you need to to make that connection.

It drives me nuts when I ask one of my team if they made the sales call I instructed them to and they confidently confirm they did - but then add the person didn't pick up, and they didn't follow up.

As I have said before, you need to be motivated to do whatever takes to achieve your goal.

So don't think your work is done because you tried to connect. Just 'doing your best' is not enough.

Unless you have made the connection and followed through until the deal is completed, you failed.

Huge rewards and little responsibility are circumstances seldom found together.

Everything in life must be finished to its complete conclusion – gym, work – the list is endless.

Don't keep spinning plates. Whether you are in the office or being a father/mother or husband/wife, if you have a task to complete, just get it done.

Make being a perfectionist your normal.

If you don't finish a task properly, it's just churning in the background and draining your energy without producing results.

Make sure you finish the task to its completion – even if you are delegating it to one of your team.

Make it your mindset to check it has been appropriately done and take ownership and responsibility to ensure it is completed correctly.

Life is all about accountability.

'The price of greatness is responsibility.' - Winston Churchill

Remember when something goes wrong, examine your role in the failure honestly because 99 per cent of the time you are the one who is responsible, so take ownership of any failures as well as success.

Judge yourself and others honestly and fairly.

When I reflect on the rollercoaster of my life, I'm now happy to admit that when something failed, the culprit was usually me.

Now I have become an accountability freak, and I make sure every base is covered.

Failure is not even an option.

I am not going to be a failure through lack of attention or due diligence because I own those decisions and actions.

NEVER ASSUME

There is no word in the world I hate more than assume – it makes an Ass out of U and Me.

I hate it so much that I have banned it in my office and in my life.

I have built an energy filter that is triggered by any threatening negativity – whatever its source.

When I hear certain words and phrases being used, I am highly sensitive to their impact.

They give me an insight into how other people are thinking, and I know that will directly affect how they will act.

To assume something means you have not checked that it is right and complete. You are shirking responsibility, and that leads to things falling apart.

Don't use the word and never assume anything!

Why? Because it's the mother of all failure!

To 'assume' means you are lazy and careless because you didn't check the job was done right or you didn't bother to check the facts.

'You cannot escape the responsibility of tomorrow by evading it today.' - Abraham Lincoln

Accountability is everything because lack of accountability produces failure.

Do you do all your due diligence and stay on top of your projects?

If not, you have happily handed your responsibility to someone else. Therefore, you have lost control of your project or even the direction of your life.

That is an epic fail – you will never be exceptional with that attitude.

Please remember assumption is the mother of all disaster.

If you were jumping out of a plane, would be happy to assume your parachute works or would you check it yourself just to make sure?

If you were going to war, would you just to assume your body armour is bulletproof?

No, when your life depends on it, you check it yourself.

Well your life depends on your attitude, so don't be slack when it comes to checking that everything is done to ensure success.

Ban the word 'assume' from your vocabulary and realise now the importance of the words you say and the words you think.

Change your words and change your world.

Take control of every aspect of your life.

Start now!

CONTROL YOUR INNER VOICE

Remember, when you are talking, you are also listening to yourself!

Your inner voice and the conversations you have in your head will control your levels of motivation.

As I have repeatedly advised, you need to change your words and change your world.

How you speak to yourself, (and others) will impact on the outcome of whatever you are doing.

We should all aspire to be the motivating partner, managing director, parent or coach.

Because what's the alternative?

Nothing good will ever flow from doom and gloom, and 'poor me' talk.

You need to quickly recognise your own negative self-talk as it will demotivate your need for immediate action.

Stop yourself whenever you think that you can't do something or aren't up to the challenge.

Then think through the steps that would allow you to confront the challenge and succeed.

Think about the internal conversation of your mind – are you often saying 'I can't do that' or 'I'm a failure,'?

Are you limiting your potential by convincing yourself you don't deserve success?

Are you listening to other people tell you that you don't deserve success?

Are you assessing your challenges as just problems instead of seeing the opportunities?

Are you generating negative or positive energy in your thought process?

Negative talk has the power to kill positive dreams. You cannot live a positive and productive life if your mind is full of negativity.

151

For example, do you say I am poor and in debt – or do you say I am just not earning enough yet?

Think about which version of this sentence is more likely to motivate you to work harder.

They both mean the same thing, yet the latter is filled with ambition, optimism and momentum.

The language you use and the way you frame the questions are essential when it comes to turning potential negative energy into positive action.

You have the power within you to change the conversation in your mind.

No matter what you are faced with in every situation in life, there is always a positive side – sometimes you need to dig deep to see it but trust me, it is there.

The difference between being exceptional and mediocre is your ability to accept this fact and always look for the positive.

Two key ingredients to being exceptional are an unwavering belief in yourself and always being motivated to drive yourself forward no matter whatever the challenges – how little sleep, what the weather is like, even a global pandemic! - there are no valid excuses to wallow in self-pity.

When you feel demotivated by negative self-talk, use the SOS system to break the cycle:

Stop – mentally tell yourself to end the negativity in your head.

Observe – think about what you are saying and how it makes you feel.

Shift – you emotional and cognitive response to the positive.

CHOOSE YOUR WORDS CAREFULLY

Don't be a victim of your own negative energy as this can be a big a drain on your motivation.

If you want to increase your levels of motivation, the process starts in your head.

When you have positive conversations in your head, it boosts your physical and mental wellbeing.

It fills you with hope and optimism, and it boosts your confidence which will have a positive effect on your performance.

When you actually think about it, your version of the world exists entirely in your mind.

That means you have complete control over your every action and reaction.

There is no universal objective truth, and therefore every piece of information is essentially propaganda.

So you can always decide the message to be promoted.

That's a powerful position to be in because it means you can shape your experience of the world entirely through your attitude.

Sometimes the madness and chaos exist in a vast bullshit bubble inside your head, so pull out the imaginary pin, burst that imaginary bubble and end your negative thinking.

The architecture of your inner world is created by the words that you use to explain and interpret every situation you experience.

So think about the vocabulary you use.

It is positive, upbeat and optimistic?

Does it exude enthusiasm and energy?

What you say is the outward projection to the world of your inner thoughts and attitude, and that is why you need to work hard to keep motivation up at all times.

You also need to have a way to carefully monitor what words come out of your mouth.

An excellent exercise to help you become more aware and mindful of how you speak to yourself and others is to set up a mental filter.

This internal filter exists in your mind but very soon becomes part of your life.

Become so aware of what energy and motivation surround you.

Write down all the negative self-criticisms that you run through your head, probably without even realising it.

Now imagine you were saying those same things to another person.

Do you think they would feel motivated by your running commentary of criticisms?

See now why your internal dialogue is so important!

I am very aware of motivation levels because I need to keep my sales team and staff full of positivity and hungry for success.

No matter what the environment – whether it's a wet week in February or a global pandemic – motivation is a way of life –not something you drop in and out of.

When I am chairing a performance meeting or a training session with them, I don't sugar-coat my criticisms if the team are failing in their objectives, but I also reward and praise their successes.

I send them out of the meeting with positive words on a high because I know how they feel will shape their motivations.

If you need a positivity boost, go back and read your gratitude list as this will help you focus on the good things that are happening in your life and convert your negative thoughts to positive ones.

Do you realise having a roof over your head and access to food and clean water puts you at an advantage to many people on the planet?

BE A POSITIVITY MAGNET

Here's the harsh truth – when people say 'Good morning, how are you?', they are just being polite, and they don't really care about your reply.

It's just a verbal device to start a productive conversation.

So be upbeat and optimistic from the outset.

When you start with a positive response, it sets the tone for the whole conversation.

154

It's also useful to remember that when you are enjoying life, you should reach out positively to other people.

Every interaction counts. You have no idea how what you say and how you say it impacts on others.

So if a co-worker, client or customer asks that question don't launch into a long list of your personal problems.

Simply respond with a positive affirmation to make them feel good about interacting with you.

Keep them motivated to want to be in your company.

They will feed off your contagious positivity, and that is always very conducive for a productive encounter.

Keep your internal and external dialogue positive and full of potential and energy.

There are no 'poor me' billionaires!

But be mindful not to lie to yourself and provide excuses for failure.

You need to own those bad decisions in the same way you own your success. Utilise every experience as growth in learning.

Don't dwell negatively on these failures or mistakes.

Leave your baggage at the door. Don't speak negative words about your past when they aren't even relevant.

This gives old problems new life.

Unplug from negativity and build a reputation for being a positive person with a can-do attitude.

To sum up, the best way to stimulate your motivation is to dream about the future and imagine yourself as already being exceptional.

Visualise yourself basking in the glow of success – see yourself earning all the money you want, achieving your goals or even standing in the church with the partner of your dreams.

Find your real motivation to make this happen.

For example, picture yourself proudly walking your daughter down the aisle on her wedding day.

To do this, you need to live long enough and be healthy, right?

So there's your real motivation to stop smoking.

Conjure up the image of walking along a tropical beach at sunset with the lover of your dreams.

There's your motivation for working hard not just to pay for the trip but also to make your relationship work so your vision will be a wonderful experience when it does happen.

There's no point investing all of your time into making money to finance the trip if you and your lover are not in a good place and end up arguing by the time you even get to the beach!

Balance your dreams and your actions in an intelligent way to achieve your goals.

FLICK THE SWITCH

Being able to recover quickly is an essential part of self-motivation.

Remember, it is not about how hard you can hit, its more about your ability to keep getting back up and fighting on until you win.

On good days, I work hard. On difficult days, I work even harder.

That's because I know when you take the inevitable knock, you need to stay utterly motivated and focused on the end goals.

It's not about losing a battle; it's about winning the war.

When you feel yourself going into a motivation nosedive, learn to flick the switch in your mind to change your outlook quickly.

Stop yourself descending into a spiral of negativity.

The small incidents can derail your good intentions because you are distracted by something insignificant.

For some people, stubbing their toe on the edge of the bed when they get up in the morning can ruin their whole day!

For average people, bad news can easily set a nasty tone for the rest of their day, and this demotivates them unnecessarily.

Perhaps you are sitting in a meeting, and you don't take in vital information because you are still thinking about the guy who cut you up in traffic on the way to work?

Maybe your tone sounds unfriendly when you are on a sales call because you are annoyed that your partner snapped at you over breakfast?

Are you for real?

The best way to stop a raging inferno from taking hold and destroying everything before it is to extinguish it as soon as it starts.

You are exceptional, so you are going to knock that petty attitude out of your mind before it has a chance to do any damage.

You have the power to flip or keep whatever thoughts are in your head.

You must always be your own gatekeeper when it comes to stress, conflict and pressure.

Before you check your phone for emails and texts, do your positive morning rituals of exercise, goal statements and gratitude.

Do this routine before anything else, because one negative piece of communication could throw you a curveball when you are tired, disorientated and vulnerable.

So avoid all distractions until you are mentally ready to deal with your problems in a positive way.

You need to focus on your fitness regime, goal statements and gratitude on your own in a quiet place.

This ritual is the equivalent of putting on your mental armour before you face the battles of the day.

I deal with any negativity in my head by imagining my brain like a pinball machine.

When I feel a negative thought coming in, I instantly flick it away.

I don't permit it even to enter my brain.

Please remember whether it's a person or a thought – something can only bother you if you give it permission – it's as clear as that.

SHIFTING POWER PLATES

The whole way through this book, I have focused on how to build your energy and use positivity to make it work for you.

But you also need to be aware of how your mind can play tricks on you to the point where it will directly impact on your mood in a negative way - even when you are experiencing the most significant success you have ever enjoyed.

Achieving success and managing success requires different skills.

Once you are aware of why the downers occur, you will be ready to control them.

Be aware of these negative feelings in response to achievement can impact on you as a person and derail your progress.

Maybe you have just achieved a goal you were working hard towards, and you expect to feel amazing and elated, but instead, you are emotionally flat - even depressed.

After all the time and energy you have invested, this is not the feeling you expect when you achieve the success you want so much.

But trust me, this is natural.

In fact, it is a sure sign you are growing and going through a period of positive transition.

Success is a journey, not a destination.

You need to travel up mountains and down the other side to progress.

It's all about highs and lows—the higher the mountain, the lower the valley.

So when you get a massive high by completing your plans, often there's a crashing low that comes after the short euphoria of success.

158

Life is a rollercoaster, and that's what makes it fun!

To really enjoy the ride, you need to understand and trust what is coming. Knowing and embracing the fact that lows naturally follow highs will empower you.

That's all just part of the process, and once you realise this, you will learn to anticipate the low and have strategies to pivot your feelings.

So why does this occur?

Surely achieving success will generate feelings of joy and satisfaction?

Well, no, not always.

You need to be fully aware of this because it can knock you seriously out of alignment.

There is biological science behind this.

Let me explain - in anticipation of reward, the brain releases dopamine.

This hormone creates feelings of both motivation and happiness.

So when you are working towards a goal you know you are going to smash, your brain is flowing out the feel good chemicals.

Each milestone you achieve gives you another dopamine hit, which makes you want to keep going with the job. But as soon as you reach your goal, that release of dopamine drops.

Ironically, you can become physically and emotionally immune to the rewards of success the more you achieve.

On a biological level, it actually becomes harder for you to to experience the same levels of joy.

Remember, the warrior loves the heat of battle because that's when they really shine.

They get to use all their skills and training as they fight. Attributes they have spent years working on.

They respond positively to the burning adrenaline of combat.

High-stress situations and the rush they produce can be addictive.

But when the constant sense of urgency comes to an abrupt halt, we experience withdrawal symptoms as the natural feel-good chemicals subside.

Like warriors, rarely do people think beyond the engagement of battle.

They don't visualise the victory because they are so focused on the war and what they need to do to win.

If you are an energetic, outgoing, brave person who is willing to do anything to achieve success, then naturally you are going to crave the high of playing the game.

The real hustler loves the chase.

The win at the end is just a bonus.

When the chase is complete, it's easy to feel a bit deflated because the adrenaline-fueling part of the process is over.

When you get what you want, you have won.

The race is finished, and you are the champion.

But what happens if it's the racing aspect you enjoy?

What if you thrive and flourish through the sheer excitement of competing?

What if victory feels a bit flat?

Let's use an example from motorsport to think about this in detail.

No matter how much fun it is to lift the trophy and spray champagne over your teammates, do you think it's the part Formula One drivers enjoy most?

Do you imagine they get the same level of excitement picking up the silverware at the end of the race as they do in the seconds sitting on the starting grid waiting for the chequered flag to go up?

Will their hearts be pounding and their adrenaline buzzing as they step up to the podium as much as when they take a bend at 180mph?

No, of course not.

The real excitement comes in the chase, and when that is over, it can leave you feeling flat. You need to be aware of that.

Make sure you always have an array of exciting projects that you are working on so you can keep your energy and motivation levels up once you strike off a goal statement as completed.

Sometimes, you can feel more than a little flat after a huge success – I mean seriously depressed.

You need to be ready to deal with that, so it does not derail you from achieving your goals.

Let me share with you a personal story to illustrate what I mean.

Recently, I worked hard for and then achieved a lifelong travel ambition. I felt great satisfaction to tick that experience off my Dream Board and goal statement list!

It was a pleasure, rather than a business trip, and that made it even more special because I could relax and enjoy it.

My beautiful and happy wife accompanied me as we left for the vacation of a lifetime.

In that beautiful moment, I felt like I had achieved something that I had worked hard my whole life to have.

I imagined that glow of satisfaction would last for days – if not weeks.

Next day after the flight, I found myself standing on the beach in Athens, and I just wanted to cry.

I was surrounded by everything I ever wanted and worked for, and yet I found myself experiencing a major downer.

I didn't know why.

So I used my own DREAM system (Determination, Re-generation, Energization, Ambition and Motivation) to pull myself out of the nosedive of negativity.

I picked myself up and carried on.

I doubled my efforts in terms of generating positivity and focus on my goals.

But this incident really resonated with me.

The feelings it stirred up disturbed me.

161

I needed to understand why, after achieving my goals, I felt like crap.

Why was I feeling so bad when I was doing so well?

I put the experience down to a one-off thing.

Perhaps, I was just having a rare off day?

Maybe I was tired and thinking about too many things?

I moved on and forgot about it.

Then the same thing happened again.

A few days after I brought a new vehicle home, I was suddenly struck how flat I felt owning it.

Something was definitely off because I wanted this car my whole life.

I had a picture of that car on my dream board for over a year.

I had included my desire to own it in every goal statement session I did.

And here, sitting on my driveway, was my dream come true.

And yet something inside was stopping me feeling the appropriate level of joy and satisfaction I knew I deserved.

So what was wrong with me?

I was genuinely concerned, so I talked these feeling of negativity and depression over with my coach Daniel.

He reassured me that these feelings of a being low after engineering your success were natural and experienced by many high achievers.

It is something he has seen many times with his top-flight clients.

In fact, when it happens now, he cheers and shakes my hand because it indicates progress.

It's the shifting tectonic plates of your mind trying to adjust to your new level of success.

If you do feel wrong, empty or even disappointed when you reach your biggest goals, **CONGRATULATIONS** because what you are experiencing is personal growth!

162

These are the psychological growing pains of becoming a success.

It's similar to the physical pain you get in your muscles when you are training your body.

If it hurts, you know your workouts are successful because you are working muscles in your body that are not used to it.

You know if you stick at it, you will soon see physical change as you sculpt your body.

Your mind works the same way. It can take time to adjust to being a winner.

Trust me, change, even for the better, is never easy.

That's because staying in your comfort zone means staying comfortable.

The temptation is to rest there and just be satisfied in your own self-imposed limitations.

So remember, if you do hit a downer, it's normal and natural.

It is a real sign that you are transforming into a different person.

Picture a butterfly emerging from its chrysalis after transforming from a caterpillar.

It has to push and struggle to break free from what it was before.

After fighting its way out, the butterfly must rest and take stock of its new reality before it can beat its wings and fly for the first time.

As you progress through my DREAM system, you are going through a similar transition with the goal of becoming something new and improved.

You need to take everything in your life apart – how you think, how you feel about yourself, how you plan and take action to change yourself into a more prosperous and happier person.

That is not is easy, and as the old saying goes – no pain, no gain!

Birth is painful, but so is rebirth.

But remember, any negative feelings are being generated in your mind.

As long as you are aware of this, you hold the power to change your thoughts.

The old you, who was comfortable in the space where they were, is trying to hold you back.

It is wrestling with you and making you feel bad, so you question your core motivations.

Your brain is withholding your mental rewards because it doesn't yet know how to process the new person you have transformed into.

It's still processing how to handle the new level you occupy.

Now your mind recognises that you are going to push yourself to even more significant challenges.

Your intense motivation levels are making it nervous because it fears it can't go up a level.

It's lagging behind the new you like an anchor trying to slow your progress.

Therefore, the downer happens to put the brakes on your ambitions because your inner self is fearful that if you aim for even higher goals, you might fail.

The mind is trying to introduce self-doubt because that is the first step on the road to giving up.

In Forbes magazine, Melody Wilding described it like this, **'Expecting your goal's future success triggers the brain's reward centres, producing a soothing feeling. This feeling continues, and you adjust to it, so much so that when you meet your goal, it's less satisfying than expected. And this can develop into an endless cycle of searching for what will make you happy, chasing goal after goal and reinforcing self-doubt.'**

It may sound counterintuitive, but after a major success, you need to be ready to feel demotivated and possibly even a bit depressed.

That empty feeling is recognised in psychology as 'the arrival fallacy'.

It's natural and normal, so you need to get over it.

If you don't recognise and master your low points, you can get caught in an incredibly self-destructive spiral.

MANAGE YOUR EMOTIONS

It is important to understand that it's very difficult to consciously control your emotions because these primal responses come from the need to survive.

You are constantly moving between different states of emotional energy which are changing in response to what you are doing, thinking and feeling.

If you are used to operating at a high energy level and then experience a fall in activity, such as weekends or holidays, this can come as a shock to the system.

You suddenly drop off the cliff from high energy positivity to low energy negativity and this can trigger anxiety, frustration and depression.

Unchecked it will quickly escalate into high energy negativity.

I experienced this recently when I was taking a break over the Christmas holidays and it made me realise that I can't just go from constant stimulation and flowing adrenalin to nothing.

It probably won't come as a huge surprise to you that I work at a million miles per hour.

That's my energy and my personality, and that's why I get so much done.

Some people find it challenging to work with me because they can't match my energy levels.

But I make no apologies for my high-intensity attitude and positivity.

I have worked hard to cultivate this energy, and I continue to work hard every day to maintain it.

If others can't keep up with me, that's fine because I only want to work with people who can match or even exceed my energy levels.

Previously, I explained how I hit a downer when I was on holiday in Athens, despite being fully aware of my achievements and success.

I used the DREAM system and very quickly fought my way out of it back up to my usual high levels of super positivity.

I worked with my coach and realised that after high achievement, energy levels can drop.

I learned to expect this and work through it when it inevitably happens.

But, this unusual episode bothered me, and I wanted to understand why it happened and how to prepare for it should it occur again.

Towards the end of 2020, I was working intensely opening new apartment sites across the UK and chasing multiple leads and opportunities.

I was smashing through challenges, and success was following my way with abundance.

I was constantly in the High Positivity Zone and loving every minute of it.

So, the day before Christmas Eve, I stopped working for the holidays and headed home to sit on the couch and enjoy the break, the same way as most people do.

For the first 48 hours, my mood was great as I enjoyed the time with my family, but suddenly I crashed and felt terrible.

I had entered the Low Negativity Zone.

As time went on this vibe began to cloud my mind. Luckily, my high level of self-awareness sounded an alarm bell as low negativity started to turn into high negativity.

I was baffled because I am usually a super positive person and was determined to immediately stop with transition and find out what was causing it.

I needed to find an answer, so I contacted my coach Daniel, and we met in my new boardroom to explore the issue.

I talked him through the rollercoaster of emotions I had experienced over the festive period, and he listened and made notes.

Then Daniel took a piece of paper and drew this diagram.

Within 90 seconds of seeing this, I understood precisely what had happened to make me feel so low.

Let me introduce you to the energy mood matrix.

High Positivity	**High Negativity**
Low Positivity	**Low Negativity**

This energy jolt throws me out of alignment. I just can't go from a million miles per hour to a dead stop where I have nothing to do.

My learning from this is that it's possible for me to enjoy holidays and work breaks but only if I have something else to occupy my mind and keep my energy in alignment.

It could be something as simple as power-washing the driveway at home, reorganising my filing system, reading or even writing up notes for my new book.

For my brain to adjust and function properly, I always need to be doing something active – albeit low energy but positive.

When I say active, I don't necessarily mean work but if you are a high-intensity achiever, you need to keep busy at all times or your mind won't be able to cope with coming to a sudden stop.

It's like slamming the brakes on a the car for an unexpected emergency stop.

The breaks will lock up, the engine will stall and suddenly you are out of control.

To stick with the analogy of the supercar, it is important to keep finely-tuned engines turned over and used regularly because they are designed and built to move.

Leave such a car parked up, unused and it will soon seize up and its performance tuning will get out of sync.

And so it is with the high achiever's brain – you must keep it ticking over at all times, even when you pull off the race track of life for a maintenance pit-stop.

So my winning solution is to be aware of your emotional states and manage the transition so that you can actively and in a controlled way move from high positivity to low positivity to keep your high performance mind ticking over.

But now I know about these different emotional states, I can actively influence how I feel and even prepare in advance.

Now you are aware of this emotional matrix, figure out your personal triggers and prepare in advance to avoid them.

For example, do you get frustrated and irritable when you are bored?

Then make sure you always have a range of high and low energy activities to occupy your mind.

Do you tend to catastrophise when you are tired? Then defer planning and decisions until you are refreshed and rested.

Try to manage your feelings and instead take a controlled and more gentle step from high positive energy to low positive energy.

It happens to everyone, so you need to be ready to power through it with extreme motivation using the strategies I'm going to share with you.

Here are some top tips to help you refocus when you experience the pain of growth and transformation:

• Remember why you are seeking achievement and success by reconnecting with what motivates you. Rediscover your original purpose.

• When you complete a task successfully, refocus your energy and honour your effort.

• Always have several different projects on the go at once.

• Share your success – praise and reward your team, offer to mentor someone else, donate to a charity, use your rewards to do good for others.

• Reflect on your past, don't regret it. Pick yourself up, dust yourself down and focus on the next goal.

• Create power statements and repeat your mantra often: 'I deserve my success'.

• Read, watch or listen to things that motivate you.

• Create a mental barrier to external negativity with positive self-talk.

• Don't seek approval from other people. Praise yourself.

• Don't take criticism from people you wouldn't ask for advice.

• Don't let the attitude of others sabotage your feeling of accomplishment.

• Don't compete with other people. Compete only with yourself.

• Stop feeling guilty for doing what is right for you.

• Enjoy your success regardless of what others think.

• Talk through your feelings openly with your mentor or someone you really trust.

• Surround yourself with successful people who support and celebrate your achievements.

• Keep a list of your accomplishments and reflect on the hard work you put in to achieve them.

• Get started right away on the next task. The sooner you get your mind off what's getting you down, the sooner it goes away.

• Remember, it's the journey that matters, not the destination. Enjoy the process, not just the outcome.

• Be grateful for the pain because it proves you are growing as a person.

• Work through self-limiting fear.

THE LONE WOLF

When you cut free of the pack, be prepared to deal with feelings of guilt.

Learn to understand and deal with it before it gets a chance to demotivate you.

Guilt can hold you back, or it can show you what you need to change.

169

Learn to tell the difference between guilt that is appropriate, i.e. when you do something that goes against your moral code, and the guilt that is given to you by someone else who wants to deflect from their inadequacies.

It would be best if you faced the reality that there are going to be casualties as you progress to success.

There are people who you are going to have to part ways with on your journey to fulfil your potential.

As you begin to see yourself and your world differently, you will also start to notice changes in others around you.

You may need to lose the wrong friends and even the wrong enemies.

Disconnect from any family members who block your path and even partners who hold you back.

You must leave the negative people of the past behind and walk away from your old pack.

You need to become a lone wolf.

The most challenging journey you will make is the one you walk alone. But that's the path that will make you strongest.

The price of being a sheep is boredom.

The cost of being a wolf is loneliness.

You must choose one or the other.

Here's the harsh truth – you might love your family and friends, but if they are failing at life, you can't save them from themselves.

You can't live their lives for them and make things better. So don't even try.

Focus on your own life and build the skills and resilience you need to survive and thrive.

A pack mentality thrives on drama, and some people love that distraction.

But listen to me now – all successful people know that 30-seconds caught up in someone else's drama, is 30 seconds of your life gone.

Even wasting 30 seconds is unacceptable to those who are driven to be exceptional.

Wasted time is worse than wasted money.

Did you know there are 86,400 seconds in every day – everyone on earth gets precisely the same amount.

What separates successful people from the rest of the pack is how motivated they are not to waste productive time.

Imagine if you just focused on earning £1 every second of every day – it wouldn't take you too long to become very rich.

'Time is an ever-decreasing commodity. When you use it up, no matter what you do, it is never given back to you.' - Robert Rivers

Don't waste the valuable commodity of time. Remain motivated by making every waking moment uber-productive.

The world's most incredible sales trainer Grant Cardone believes saying that you don't have time is the biggest lie you tell yourself.

It is the number one excuse that people give for not accomplishing all the things they want.

So create the time. Plan your schedule with military precision and design out the unproductive downtime.

Be obsessed with squeezing out every valuable minute in the day. Every moment can be a step on the journey of success if you use it wisely.

Develop a tight, disciplined schedule which is structured to maximise productivity in every part of your day.

For example, if I have an early morning flight to a business meeting, I will get a taxi, so I can make calls and take notes first thing in the morning.

I transform my journey to the airport into productive time so when I am at work, I am actually working all the time and squeezing every bit of value out of the day.

As I explained before, everybody has the same amount of time in the day, it's how you use it that counts.

When I arrive at the terminal, I check in, find a quiet place and get on my phone to respond to emails and make more calls.

On the flight, I will read or do research. I go to my meeting and conduct the business I need to do, then repeat the process on the journey back.

I focus on working towards my goals, and that means constant calls, correspondence and meetings to move my projects forward.

I fill my time productively so that you can see that I don't have time for toxic drama from negative people.

Don't feel guilty for being a person who prioritises getting things done over endless discussion or even worse – bitching.

Avoid the merchants of doom who see only problems and disaster.

If that is their mindset, then they will never succeed.

If a ship is sinking, the best advice is to dive off and swim away before you get pulled under with it.

You drowning in other people's negativity and drama as well will not benefit anyone.

Especially not you!

When you start to transform into someone different, it probably won't suit everyone in your life and those people will try to sabotage your confidence.

To be successful means you are naturally going to stand out from the crowd.

Some people around you will try to discourage you.

Sometimes for the wrong reasons such as jealously or resentment or even with honourable intentions.

The person may be just trying to protect you because they don't understand or share your levels of motivation.

People will tell you to slow down and not be so ambitious.

But here is my personal tip – don't take any advice from people who have not achieved exceptional success that outstrips even your own achievements.

If you scratch around with chicken, you will cluck. If you fly with eagles, you will soar.

It takes courage and self-determination to leave behind colleagues, friends and even family members.

Becoming a lone wolf takes bravery because you are stepping outside and away from your protective pack.

So be warned, as you grow and transform you are going to experience a strong desire to remain where you are and blend into the herd.

That feels safe and easy, but it also means that you won't progress as your forward momentum has stopped.

But if you give in to this feeling, you will never be exceptional.

Embrace the fact that sometimes achievement and success can bring short-lived feelings of guilt and depression.

Your success can cause shockwaves for those around you because they have become used to you being one particular way, and they struggle to cope when you transform into something better.

Believe me, when the haters turn up, you know you are doing something right!

Take strength in the fact that haters don't really hate you; they hate themselves.

They project hate onto you because you're an image of what they want to be.

Seeing you achieve goals they can't achieve or are too lazy even to try makes them feel uncomfortable.

They target you to make up for their own failings.

'A truly strong person does not need the approval of others any more than a lion needs the approval of sheep.' - Vernon Howard

Your development as a person threatens the established pecking order – especially if you are changing from being a passive follower to a pro-active leader.

Your personal growth can be threatening for many people.

They might respond with judgment, rejection and even ridicule.

To be successful, you must expect this and be ready to reject it.

Learn to rise above those who want to drag or keep you down at their level.

You are on a different mission now in life – the old you has gone.

The unsatisfactory life you were living before is over.

You are destined for massive success because you have committed yourself to work hard to achieve it.

Don't let somebody else hold you back – even if it's a loved one – you need to let it go.

You have a simple choice: let the guilt compel you back to conformity or reject the responsibility and embrace your success?

Your success will impact on other people in ways you can't even imagine.

It may even impact your personal relationship if your partner is uncomfortable with how you are mentally changing.

Your new assertiveness or even your increased opportunities to travel and meet new people might be hard for them to handle.

But that comes from their insecurities, not yours.

You are under no obligation to stifle your success to pander to other people's lack of motivation.

Too many people downplay their accomplishments because the people they associate with haven't achieved great things.

If this is the case for you, then you are hanging out with the wrong people.

If you hunt with kings and queens – you become royalty.

Buzz around with barflies - you become a loser.

In the cold light of day – if you are serious about being successful, then you just can't be a people pleaser.

Here's why. People are only happy when you tell them what they want to hear.

This often involves having to tell lies to make them feel better.

Lies lead to mistakes and missed opportunities.

You end up carrying the can for other people's failures.

If you do this, you have allowed people to book you on to a guilt trip to make up for their lack of motivation and action.

Stop apologising right now for your success.

Use only positive talk to let your subconscious mind know that it is safe and right for you to be successful.

Focus on how amazing your life is and drop the heavy baggage.

Your life is a journey, and you need to work hard to take every positive step forward, so don't burden yourself with the weight of other people's expectations.

Build up your self-confidence by celebrating what you have achieved and rewarding yourself when you reach a goal.

Moving forward, you now know that feeling guilty is a natural part of being successful because exceeding your peer group's achievements defies the natural rules of pack mentality.

Do not let negative feelings created in your mind or by those around you demotivate you.

Stop feeling guilty for the success you have worked so hard to achieve.

You are changing as a person, but very often people around you cannot adapt to that change.

Understand their negativity for what it is – a failure on their behalf – not yours.

The caterpillar is always jealous of the butterfly, especially if it cannot accept that it also has the power to change into something better.

When you feel low or demotivated, say this sentence out loud – 'I am worthy of my success because I have worked hard work to get it'.

As I am making my goal statements, I have a daily mantra that starts with the phrase - I am.

Every day I say these sentences out loud, so both the universe and I know the script for the day.

I am a total success and positivity magnet.

I am a huge money and vast wealth maget.

I am a total health and fitness maget.

I am dedicated to doing whatever it takes to achieve my goals.

I am a loving dad.

I am a loving husband.

These are my personal motivations, but the list can be endless.

You need to choose what messages you send out about who you are and what you want to be.

What are you going to say after I am...?

FEELING DEMOTIVATED?   DO IT ANYWAY

Fear is a powerful motivating force.

But unless you know how to harness it and, more importantly, how to conquer it, it can be limiting and paralysing.

Nothing makes us more uncomfortable than fear.

That's why it's such a good motivator but only when you take control of it.

If fear has hold of you, then it is like an anchor tied to your ambitions.

And we have so many fears: fear of pain, disease, injury, failure, not being accepted, missing an opportunity or even being scammed.

Fear invokes the flight or fight system, and our first reaction is often to flee back to our comfort zone.

But that is a big mistake. You have worked hard to move beyond where you are comfortable.

You need to accept that for progress to be made, you are going to have to go over, around or even through the things that are stopping or limiting you.

Remember **'Fortune favours the brave.'**

Boldness is a necessary part of courage, but it must be based on an intelligent assessment of the potential risks and rewards.

Thoughts translated into action leads almost invariably to positive results. But that process can be interrupted by the fear you don't even know that you have.

Every significant venture in the history of man has begun with faith and a giant leap into the unknown.

General Douglas MacArthur once said, **'There is no security in life, only opportunity.'**

Giving in to what you fear will stop you from grabbing potentially-lucrative opportunities because you are clinging to the fake lifeboat of security.

I consider myself a brave person who always tries to stare fear in the face and push on through it until I knock it out.

Maybe that is directly linked to growing up in a conflict situation where any sign of fear was seen as a weakness that could be exploited.

Wherever my bravery comes from, it is the baseline foundation for my success because I will always go further with my plans than anyone who fancies themselves as my competition.

Some people want it to happen; some wish it would happen; others make it happen.

Which type of person are you? Because to make things happen, you must be prepared to do what it takes – no matter how it makes you feel.

This is an excellent time to take stock of what you actually fear – not in an abstract way but by drawing up a list of all those negative thoughts in your mind that hold you back.

You know they exist in the dark recess of your mind but bring them into the light so you can face and overcome them.

Write down what you fear most under the following categories – Relationships, Money, Career, Health, The Future.

Now you have some control over them because you have taken them out of your mind and can judge them accurately for what they are.

Use them to learn lessons about who you were in the past.

Take the negative experience that caused your fear in the first place and convert it into a motivator.

Remember that merely replaying painful experiences and memories is a form of self-abuse.

In 1987, internationally renowned author Susan Jeffries wrote a groundbreaking self-help book called 'Feel the Fear and Do It Anyway'.

In it, she identified five truths about fear:

1. The fear will never go away as long as you continue to grow! Every time you take a step into the unknown, you experience anxiety. The fear is part of the package.

2. The only way to get rid of the fear of doing something is to go out and…do it! When you do it often enough, you will no longer be afraid in that particular situation. You will have faced the unknown, and you will have handled it.

3. The only way to feel better about yourself is to go out and…do it! With each little step you take into unknown territory, a pattern of strength develops. You begin feeling healthier and stronger.

4. Not only are you afraid when facing the unknown, so is everyone else! This should be a relief. You are not the only one out there feeling fear. Everyone feels fear when taking a step into the unknown. Yes, all those people who have succeeded in doing what they have wanted to do in life have felt the fear - and did it anyway. So can you!

5. Pushing through fear is less frightening than living with the bigger underlying fear that comes from a feeling of helplessness! This is the one truth that some people have difficulty understanding. When you push through the fear, you will feel such a sense of relief as your feeling of helplessness subsides. You will wonder why you did not take action sooner. You will become more and more aware that you can truly handle anything that life hands you.

Whether it's changing careers, buying a new house or trying something new for the first time, we all feel fear when experiencing change.

From now on, say these three words when you face a new situation or challenge: I'll handle it.

What if I lose my job over this? I'll handle it.

What if my car breaks down?   I'll handle it.

What if this fight ends the friendship?   I'll handle it.

What if I fail miserably and am humiliated?   I'll handle it.

Repeat this to yourself again and again until you develop enough trust in your abilities to handle any situation that comes your way.

Fear is that voice in your head that makes you doubt your abilities.

It's so sneaky and powerful that it can distract you from achieving your potential due to an incident that happened decades ago.

Maybe at school, you were told your handwriting was terrible, or you are rubbish at sport.

Perhaps you didn't excel academically and were told you were stupid or too fat, too thin, too loud.

Maybe you were raised poor and have issues around inadequacies, or you may have experienced dysfunctional personal relationships.

Going forward, you avoid doing these things because you believed you aren't capable and don't want your weakness exposed.

That's natural, but it's also self-limiting.

What you fear exists only in the past. It is a memory that is controlling your future.

Unfortunately, the human mind can hang on to negative comments so remember to let them go.

It stores them up to give you an excuse not to try something new.

The monster dials up the pressure and the negative voice in your head to stop you growing and transitioning for success.

It does this because once you no longer listen to it and fear it, it loses all of its power to bully you into small thinking.

Every time you are winning, be prepared to fight the old you.

My learning on this is the longer you ignore fear or even actively avoid it, the worse it gets.

The problem multiplies in your head, and suddenly you are dealing with a giant angry monster that wants you to remain in your comfort zone.

It will dig its claws into your creativity and stop you from moving into the next level of success.

But remember, it does not exist outside of your mind. You are the monster, and you are the only one that can feed it.

Here is a great story that illustrates this.

One evening an old Cherokee native American told his grandson about a battle that goes on inside people.

He said, 'My son, the battle is between two 'wolves' inside us all. One is Evil. It is anger, envy, jealousy, sorrow, regret, greed, arrogance, self-pity, guilt, resentment, inferiority, lies, false pride, superiority, ego and fear. The other is good. It is joy, peace, love, hope, serenity, humility, kindness, benevolence, empathy, generosity, truth, compassion and faith.'

The grandson thought about it for a minute and then asked his grandfather: 'Which wolf wins?'

The old Cherokee simply replied, 'The one you feed.'

Let me share a recent personal example.

I was not confident or comfortable about public speaking – especially when I knew it was to be recorded and put out on social media for marketing purposes.

I wanted to introduce my fantastic new Dream Luxury Serviced Apartments site in Liverpool to the world, and I knew I was the only person who could really share the real vision of the project.

Therefore, video content from me was essential on my business social media channels.

Maybe I had a bit of a chip on my shoulder about my hard, working-class accent or perhaps I was worried about what people would think about someone successful coming from Belfast given all the previous negativity associated with my city.

I just didn't want to make the videos because I feared being judged negatively.

It was way out of my comfort zone.

So one day a few months ago, I was standing outside my fantastic new serviced apartments building in Liverpool.

I had my phone in my hand, and I wanted to film myself telling everyone about this project.

I was so proud of my team and I had achieved opening this amazing short-stay apartment block in the middle of a pandemic.

I faced my fear. Then I thought, 'today is the day that I am going to beat this fear - fuck it – I am going to do this because it is going to benefit my sales team and I'.

I filmed a short, selfie-style piece on my camera phone and posted it on social media.

I was nervous and anxious about what would happen next.

I posted it up and waited on the response.

The video got a fantastic reaction from followers, thus attracting more customers and investors.

The comments were overwhelmingly positive. Sure there were some haters – did I care?

No – because I am standing outside something my team and I worked to create while the keyboard critics are sitting in their houses doing nothing and living in fear.

We got loads of new business leads and hundreds hits on our social media pages from potential customers.

Job done!

I realised that, as US President Franklin D Roosevelt famously said, **'there is nothing to fear but fear itself.'**

The only limitations that existed were the ones I was imposing on myself.

Nobody can make you feel inferior unless you give them permission to do so.

After I smashed through that first wall of fear, I went from strength to strength, and I now post videos all the time.

They are a fantastic resource for attracting customers and interest, and I get to share my passion for business directly.

I discovered that I actually love public speaking.

I am genuinely motivated to do more of it.

I stopped worrying what other people think of me and what I have to say and I just got on with it.

They either like the videos, or they don't. They either judge me as a working-class guy from Belfast, or they don't.

I can't change or influence what they think of me. Nor do I need or want to.

That's their baggage, and I am not going to carry it for them.

I just want them to remember my brand and book my apartments.

The transaction is straightforward and stripping out the emotion made me realise that.

I looked outward at my objective, (to promote my brand for increased sales), instead of inward, (how I felt).

I focused on the practicalities of getting the job done and made the task about something else. This tricked the voice in my mind that had been telling me not to do it.

I took massive outward action to overcome an emotional obstacle that was stopping me moving to the next level of growth.

To do this, I let go of my past experiences, trusted the moment and accepted myself for who I am.

I stepped into the pain and resolved to push through it.

This small action of facing down my fear has increased my business potential, and my new freedom and confidence will open doors of opportunity for me in the future.

Fear is a key – it can both lock and unlock potential.

Facing down your fears gives you a tremendous sense of empowerment.

It can open the gates to new opportunities and help you embrace the talent and abilities that you didn't even know you possessed.

The moment you have control of the key, and you turn it in the lock to open up a new pathway, you will be filled with power and motivation to keep going to even greater heights of success.

Grant Cardone gives tremendous advice on dealing with the demotivating effects of fear.

1. Realise that everyone has fear. You don't have some unusual or rare disease that causes you and you alone to be plagued by doubt. So get over yourself.

2. Fill your calendar. Make yourself so busy that you don't have time for fear. Fear thrives on that time you give it to think about what scares you. If you don't give it any time at all, it will starve.

3. Use your fear. Whenever something scares you, do it. Move towards it. Fear is a challenge that allows you to grow. That client you've been dreading to call? Call them now.

4. GET OUT OF YOUR COMFORT ZONE! Growth can only happen when you challenge yourself.

How you responded to feeling demotivated impacts on the outcome of the challenge directly.

For example, recently, I had a hectic and stressful weekend.

Like most people, I try to use one of my weekend days to recharge my batteries properly but due to urgent business issues regarding a big deal I wanted to land I was plugged in and wired with adrenaline.

That meant I got very little rest or relaxation.

So I wake up at 4am on Monday morning and feel tired and demotivated by the massive workload over the previous few days.

I have two choices.

Hit the snooze button, pull the duvet over my head and try to go back to sleep.

That is tempting of course, but by not taking massive, positive action then nothing in my day was going to change.

But I knew I would wake up two hours later, not any better rested and now behind on my schedule.

Was that going to make me feel motivated?

No.

So it wasn't even an option.

I was not going to let the monster of doubt and anxiety in my head dictate the agenda for my day.

I could make this decision because I am massively self-aware of who I am and how I feel.

I am prepared to do whatever it takes to ensure I am performing at my optimal level. I knew I could handle it.

So instead, despite being mentally and physically exhausted, I jumped out of bed, focused on getting my attitude alignment right and hit the gym.

I smashed it so hard that I did double my training session time and bounced out on a high.

My brain fog cleared, and I had power rushing through my body.

I paid extra attention to writing my goal statements and really focused on my gratitude session.

I left for work feeling happy, full of energy and in total alignment.

I had worked through the logistics of the deal I was making and by taking control and action, was confident that I was back in charge.

I felt in a good place and was radiating positivity, so I knew I could trust the universe to deliver exactly what I needed.

By 8am, I was sitting in my office with all of my issues and challenges from the weekend sorted and ready to take on Monday and all of the new opportunities it had to offer me.

I got my coffee, answered my emails and looked out of my window across Belfast's beautiful skyline as dawn breaks and I feel proud of the changes that both the city and I have embraced for success.

At 9am, the phone rang, and I was informed the massive property deal I was working on that had been hanging in the balance on Friday afternoon had just gone through successfully.

I punched the air, and in that second I knew I had a DREAM system that worked for me and could work for other people.

I had figured out a simple method for success, and I needed to share it.

That small decision about whether to have a lie-in or get up for the next round of the fight taught me a powerful lesson about how your attitude directly determines the outcome.

All the massive achievements in life flow from the small, everyday decisions we make in the moment.

It all boils down to this - can you pick yourself up when you think you can't?

Can you get up out of bed - your first comfort zone - and start every day with a positive mental outlook?

Are you confident that you can handle it - whatever it is?

That's the time to dig deep into your psychological toolbox and figure out a way to manage your attitude.

That's when you can fall back on my DREAM system. Every point of motivation and action is in its approach.

It has worked for me every day for over a decade and it will work for you now that you know the secret.

So how did I turn that day around?

The same way I turn every day around.

I am **D**etermined to have a fantastically, productive day.

I know that releasing endorphins through exercise would **R**egenerate me at a cellular level.

I adjusted my mental attitude and focus, and the power of gratitude **E**nergised me.

I tapped into my **A**mbitions to be the best version of myself.

And I **M**otivated myself to get up, get out and hustle in the extreme for success.

In the moment of the first crucial decision of the day – to crawl back under the covers or get up and embrace the challenges – my **DREAM** came true.

I instantly made the right and productive choice because I had trained myself for the biggest struggle I face every day.

The battle is with my old, self-limiting self.

I had a framework that kicked in to intuitively guide me onto the right path.

Those five keywords – **Determination, Regeneration, Energization, Ambition and Motivation** - are my mantra for success. Now, they are also yours.

Your simple take away from all of this is, if you put the work in, results will follow.

'**In the long run, we shape our lives and we shape ourselves. The process never ends until we die. And the choices we make are ultimately or own responsibility.**' - Eleanor Roosevelt.

The more effort and belief you invest, the greater your rewards will be.

Inspired by Belfast's ability to re-imagine itself, I have shared with you my life experiences and what my home city has taught me about building personal resilience.

I have now shared all this with you and how you choose to use this knowledge will decide whether you will be fearless in the future.

Good luck on your life-long journey of personal growth and financial success and remember always to DREAM big!

Mission Statement

Live on your WITS!

Do whatever it takes!

You are the only person who can make this happen!

TOM'S TIPS FOR MOTIVATION

- Remember - success is a journey, not a destination, so every productive minute of your day counts.
- Motivation beats temptation. It's the driving force that keeps you going.
- Find out what motivates you. Is it money, fame, excellence or a desire to have power over your destiny?
- Control your inner voice. Change your words to change your world.
- Wanting something is not enough. You must hunger for it and desire it above everything else.
- Winners don't seek out excuses; they find solutions because they are so strongly motivated to succeed.
- You must push yourself because no-one is going to do it for you.
- Tough times don't last, but tough people do.
- Motivate yourself to be a doer in a world full of people who give up and never finish anything.
- Don't keep spinning plates. Finish the task properly.
- Being able to recover quickly from any setback is an essential part of self-motivation.

DREAM

Conclusion

I am so grateful that I have written this book.

It makes me proud to be able to celebrate the resilience of my city and its amazing people.

I'm genuinely thankful to highlight Northern Ireland as a motivating example of recovery from the most extreme and prolonged challenges.

And this year has certainly been full of many challenges for almost every single person on earth, not just Belfast.

When I first put pen to paper in March 2020, the COVID-19 pandemic and lock-down had just started.

Everyone was full of doom and gloom and focused on a very bleak future.

Back then, we didn't even know how long the crisis would last. We had no idea of the cost or the impact of effectively shutting down the economy for such a long period of time.

The scale of sickness and the death toll was incalculable. Every newspaper, TV show and social media post was constantly lit up with terrible statistics and grim images.

The natural response is mass panic and uncertainty as fear kicked in.

But I took a deep breath and tried a different approach.

I looked forward to a future beyond the chaos.

I trusted the Universe and the human spirit to find a solution and get us through.

Whatever was going to happen, I knew I could handle it.

I have lived through hopelessness and know there is always light at the end of the tunnel.

The critical skill is motivating yourself to walk toward that light even when you have been hit by the train.

Always remember that the knock-backs and lock-downs are all part of the journey.

188

You need to give 100 per cent or get off the track because effort and reward come in equal measure.

You need to be able to uplift and motivate the people around you.

Every single day of this global crisis, I have told my friends, my family and my teams how amazing they are.

I assured them that we are all going to get through this pandemic together and emerge stronger and better than before.

I have practised my gratitude more deeply and profoundly because I am so aware of all the things I need to be thankful for.

Success is only rented, and you need to pay the rent every day or face very swift eviction.

As I explained before, I'm not smarter, luckier or more privileged than you or anyone else.

I just worked hard and learned from my mistakes.

I was honest when it came to my own failings, and I worked hard to turn my life around.

But trust me, that's not enough if you want to be genuinely exceptional.

If you want to shine brighter and fly higher than everyone else, you must be prepared to do whatever it takes to achieve your goals.

You must live on your WITS but channel your positive energy into a strategy with time-limited goals and dreams.

Today, as I finish this final chapter, we are still under some restrictions of movement, but the first person in the UK has just received a new vaccine against COVID-19.

Coincidently, it was a sprightly 91-year-old woman who originally comes from Enniskillen in Northern Ireland!

Grandmother Margaret Keenan made the headlines today as the first person to get one of 800,000 doses of the Pfizer vaccine that will be dispensed in the coming weeks, with millions more to follow.

This medical breakthrough is the most significant sign of hope the whole world has received in over 10 months.

The world has changing, and we have adapted to the new ways of doing business.

In a way, we all need to reinvent ourselves at this point in history, so it's good to start with a tried-and-tested blueprint for success.

And that is my unique DREAM system.

Back at the start of the pandemic, I anticipated that we would come out of the crisis.

And while we are not out of the woods yet, a solution is now in place.

Determined, Regenerative, Energetic, Ambitious and Motivated people worked together to find a way to fight back.

This combination of qualities worked like a Dream.

They visualised their end goal then invested 100 x the effort typically required to fast-track their success.

In record time, brilliant doctors and virologists worked with their dedicated teams to find vaccines to combat the worst crisis humanity has faced since World War Two.

To every one of those people who sacrificed so much to save lives, I am genuinely grateful.

They are the true heroes who should inspire hope in us all.

I celebrate all the small businesses who adapted their working practices to ensure a bright, post-pandemic future for their ventures.

And the big companies that were a supply lifeline for so many people trapped in their homes shielding from infection.

My heart goes out to everyone who lost someone or something important to them during this unprecedented time of challenge and change.

So remember, when you think the odds are completely stacked against you, we got through 2020 and survived.

That's one of my main motivations for writing this book.

I really want people to know and understand the incredible power and capacity they have to make their lives everything they want them to be.

You can make your life incredible by using your mindset.

By taking control of your thoughts and your actions, you take control of your destiny.

Mindset is the key to your success.

A winning mindset can conquer everything.

I decided to write this book which is full of good energy and positivity as I am running a hospitality empire during global lock-down.

As I have said many times in this book, there are no good excuses for failure or just to give up.

If you really want to be a success, you will find a way. If you don't, you will find an excuse.

This pandemic has caused a national health crisis, but it is also an economic crisis.

But neither you nor I should let that stop our growth in both our personal and career development.

The world's billionaires did extremely well during the coronavirus pandemic, growing their already-huge fortunes to a record high of $10.2tn (£7.8tn).

A report by Swiss bank UBS found that billionaires increased their wealth by more than a quarter at the height of the crisis from April to July 2020.

Not only were they able to ride the storm but also benefitted when the stock market rebounded.

Because they have an appetite for risk and self-assured confidence, the super-wealthy could gamble some of their considerable fortunes.

"[Our clients] did not panic during the sell-down," Sergio Ermotti, UBS's chief executive told the Financial Times. "Instead, they used it to build up positions."

And that is what resilience is all about.

That applies to everyone – not just billionaires.

Invest in yourself every day, and you will soon reap the dividends.

It doesn't matter how small you start – just start.

In just five years, Grant Sabatier of Millennial Money went from having $2.26 in his bank account to $1 million.

On his blog, the 31-year-old self-made millionaire shares the single most important hack he used to build his wealth: "I break down ALL of my money goals into daily goals. I still deposit money every day into my investment accounts."

He started with the goal of setting aside $50 a day.

At first, "some days it was only $5, but I rarely missed a day," Grant says. "Then I started trying to make as much money as possible every day so that I could invest it. I stopped thinking long term and thought every day about making that $50 threshold."

His daily goal of $50 deposits soon became his daily minimum. He started setting aside $70, then $80, then $100 dollars a day… "Then as my side hustles started really taking off I started depositing $500+ a day. ... Then I put $5,000 in a day, then $20,000, and the rest is history."

So as you can see from this example, consistency and determination always pay off.

You need to have the skills, energy and insight to find every opportunity, even in a crisis.

Make sure your eggs are not in one basket, and you have multiple ways to make money.

In author Thomas Corley's five-year study of self-made millionaires, he found that many of them develop multiple streams of income: 65 per cent had three streams, 45 per cent had four streams, and 29 per cent had five or more streams.

These additional streams include property rentals, stock market investments, and part-ownership in a side business.

But don't do it because you are obsessed just with the idea of money – instead become obsessed with being so exceptional that you always achieve your goals.

Most people think the rich are obsessed with money, but most of the self-made wealthy are obsessed with success. Money is nothing more than a gauge the wealthy use to see if they've achieved their latest target.

The wealthiest people see business and life as a game they love to win.

And that is what motivates me.

I always want to be a winner even when the goalposts unexpectedly shift half-way through the game - like the onset of the pandemic.

As the world was turned upside down, I was able to fall back on experience and resilience and act to support my business not just to survive but actually to flourish.

I acted quickly and adapted my business practices to ensure the safety of both my staff and clients.

Staff motivation levels were increased through active policies and programs to support people and help them feel valued.

I went out into the market and looked for newly-emerging business opportunities and property deals.

I researched, then stepped into new markets for short-stay and staycation accommodation.

Sitting back and putting my plans on pause was not an option so I triggered my marketing team to make my brand even more visible through a greater social media presence.

I didn't sit back and use the pandemic as an excuse to fail, I used it as an excuse to expand and to get ready for the inevitable post-pandemic boom time.

I have recently announced a six-figure investment program with plans to expand into a further 10 cities Europe-wide by 2022, creating over 300 jobs across 600 new apartments.

And we are also working on new builds and deals in major cities in the UK including Manchester, Glasgow, Cardiff, Liverpool, Birmingham, Middlesbrough, Dublin, Leeds, London and Berlin.

I'm staying focused on these growth plans and not being deterred.

Dream Luxury Serviced Apartments remains committed to becoming a serious global player in the travel market with an excellent reputation for providing accommodation to both corporate and leisure clients.

We are super ready for the world beyond lock-down and fear.

Every day we get another step closer to normality so I will redouble my efforts to make sure my staff and businesses come out of this even stronger than what we went into it.

These projects and so many more are my goals being achieved and my dreams coming true.

I have so many positive and concrete plans for the future, and I can't wait to achieve every single one of them.

I work hard every day from the moment I get up until I go to bed to achieve all of the things that are important to me.

But everyone has different goals.

Maybe you want to earn a lot of money, be a sporting success, have a great relationship, write a book - whatever you want to achieve is up to you.

The path to success in what venture you choose is always the same regardless of your dream:

1: Determination

2: Regeneration

3: Energisation

4: Ambition

5: Motivation

The simple system for getting what you want out of life is in your hands right now.

You have the knowledge, and you have the power to change and grow into the person you always wanted to be.

Changes take time and effort but put in the work, and the rewards are there for the taking.

It's entirely up to you how you write the script of the rest of your life.

Now is the time to invest in yourself so you can challenge your abilities and push yourself beyond what you believe are your limitations.

I will level with you when I started this I didn't know if I could write a book.

I had never done it before, but I knew I wanted something positive to come out of this most unusual time.

So I told myself I could write a book.

I put the effort in to make it happen, and the proof of my success is that I have been able to communicate all of my experiences and learning directly to you.

I have distilled years of graft and research into a system that I know works, and I am grateful to be able to share it with you.

The whole purpose of writing this book is to share hope and help you break the shackles of fear that have been holding you back.

Now I have conquered this first writing challenge; I fully intend to author more books.

I am determined to share my knowledge and expertise on health, wealth and sales and my secrets on how to achieve them all.

I'm also going to host and organise training seminars, one-to-one elite coaching, online resources, podcasts, videos, and a long list of courses and learning innovations so we can work more directly together.

I want to personally thank you for taking the time to read my book and I hope it has helped you understand your dreams and more importantly that you have the power to achieve them. I send you all the health and positivity in the world as you travel on your journey of life.

Join my DREAM TEAM today at www.fear-less.co.uk

I personally invite you to sign up to my program for success so I can help you turn your dreams into your reality through access to my blogs, training and mentoring resources.

<u>Further Reading Suggestions</u>

The 10X Rule – Grant Cardone

Be Obsessed Or Be Average – Grant Cardone

If you're not first, you're last – Grant Cardone

Unleash The Power – Tony Robbins

This is just the beginning of your DREAM future and it's only going to get better from here!

My next book

'Whatever It Takes'

will be available Summer 2021.